RIVER

150 years of Brisbane River Housing

Cover: The Lamb residence ('Home' 1902-3)
Kangaroo Point - designed by architect Alexander
B. Wilson, sits high on the Kangaroo Point Cliffs
across the riverbend from Garden Point.

Inside front cover:
Photograph of courtesy John Oxley Library.

First Edition
ISBN 0-646-44222-8
Author Patrick Dixon
Designed by Fine Aligns Pty Ltd
Photography by Millars Photographic Service Pty Ltd
Fergies Image to Plate Printers

contents

foreword

150 years of Brisbane River Housing could not have been produced without the interest and generosity of the property owners whose homes are featured in this book. I have no doubt that many doors were opened in support of The Mater Medical Research Institute, which would have remained firmly shut for a commercial venture.

The Research Institute continues the mission of the Sisters of Mercy in caring for the sick. Since they established the Mater Misericordiae Hospital at South Brisbane in 1906, the Sisters' love and compassion over the last century have won them a place in the hearts of countless Brisbane families who have been the recipients of their kindness and care.

This goodwill, entrenched in the Brisbane community, enabled us to enlist the support of freelance photographers, who granted permission to reproduce their works, historians, and architects, all of whom have willingly given their time and expertise in support of this venture.

This book is intended as a personal observation and comment on the physical and social factors that have influenced 'River Houses', their popularity and style. It was never intended as a historical document; that is better left to two excellent publications, *The River: a Source Book for the Future* edited by Peter Davie, Errol Stock, and Darryl Low Choy and also Helen Gregory's *The Brisbane River Story*. I drew heavily from these books together with *The Moreton Bay Courier to the Courier Mail 1846 to 1992* by Geoff Gaylard and Erica Hart from which the timelines are extracted.

Hopefully this book will accomplish four things: to raise money to fight cancer; to inspire, in some small way, quality design of future river housing; to gently advise property owners that they have some responsibility to ensure that their river frontages are both appealing to the eye and respectful of the environment; to increase the resolve of Governments to continue to rejuvenate our river.

A special thanks to the *"150 years of Brisbane River Housing"* team: David Millar, Glenda Holyoake, and Jacob Aldridge, whose donations of both time and talent have made this book a reality.

Patrick Dixon

Patrick Dixon

What makes a river so restful to people is that it doesn't have any doubt
- it is sure to get where it is going, and it doesn't want to go anywhere else.

Hal Boyle

The Brisbane River snakes its way to Moreton Bay.

The Brisbane River meanders 74 kilometres across a 26 kilometre breadth of urban Brisbane.

might & majesty
Chapter One

Rivers have always held a primitive fascination for mankind. Most of the world's great cities were born on their banks. In bygone centuries, rivers were the trade routes that linked ancient civilisations, the natural borders of great empires and the highways of uncharted lands. We are drawn to their mysteries, their abundant gifts, as well as their guarantee of life-preserving water and easy access to fertile plains and food.

From Jason and the Argonauts sailing up the Bosphorous to the Goths and Huns breaching the security of the Danube to raid the Roman Empire, and Washington crossing the Delaware in the winter to advance American independence, the history of human civilisations is inextricably linked to its rivers.

The world has many great rivers including the Amazon, the Mississippi, the Nile, the Danube, the Yangtze, and the Irrawaddy. Over time, these have all been romanticised by poets, songwriters, and storytellers, developing their own self-perpetuating legends, their own mystique, which is often at the core of a city's self-consciousness. The Mississippi can thank Mark Twain; the Nile, the Pharaohs; the Amazon, the Hollywood film studios; the Tigris

"Middenbury House" (1865) Toowong - once the home of Thomas Finney, co-founder of successful department store Finney Isles Co Ltd. Photograph by Richard Stringer.

and Euphrates, the Bible and Koran; and the great rivers of Europe were immortalised by Mozart, Da Vinci, and Tennyson.

A river is always the heart of a city. Residents can draw on its beauty for conscious pondering or free-form dreaming. The more active find avenues of recreation, while others are content to while away time imbibing its natural beauty.

The Brisbane River was, when discovered, without doubt as scenic as any. The lower reaches of the river were fringed by both open forest and rainforest, including towering hoop pines rising to more than 160 feet. Upstream and along the broader flood plains, rainforests changed abruptly to open eucalypt forest with a grassy understory, swamp oak, river oak and weeping bottlebrush. The river was alive with ducks, fish, and black swans. Its beauty left many early travellers lost for words. Although initial descriptions were in journal form and largely objective, the authors' awe could often not be contained. The river scenery and

reaches were described variously as "beautiful", "pretty", "picturesque", "noble", even "magnificent". Early explorers had found themselves a veritable "Garden of Eden", on an otherwise seemingly hostile continent.

The Brisbane River was a long, large, deep river, flanked by rainforest, sandstone, and ironstone cliffs, and bordered by alluvial plains. It was obviously an ideal site for a major settlement. When the Governor of New South Wales Sir Thomas Brisbane travelled some twenty-eight miles upstream in 1824, a year after the river's discovery by John Oxley, he was excited by what he saw, hence the birth of Brisbane.

Several generations have passed since free settlement began along the banks of our river. The transformation that has taken place is staggering, and many feel this is more a matter for condolence than congratulation. Hindsight is a wonderful friend, and our forefathers forged ahead as best they knew, ignorant of the damage they would do to this unique eco-system. As with all great things, while there is life there is hope. European people's early impact on the river is now being reversed and we are seeing the rejuvenation of this great river that now enjoys the love and support of our community. For a river that has been traced back to Early Tertiary times, perhaps even into the Mesozoic Era more than 65 million years ago, and which was home to the Aboriginal people for many thousands of years, white man's history on it exists in just a blink of an eye.

The Brisbane River is arguably the most important waterway along the 15 000 kilometres of Australia's eastern coastline. The urban section extends for 80 kilometres, from its mouth to Colleges Crossing. Then our great waterway continues a further 140 kilometres

dissecting Toogoolawah and Kilcoy to the north-west where it is flanked by the Great Dividing Range, the Conondale Range, and the D'Aguilar Range. Its catchment area spreads from near Nanango in the north-west to the foothills of Toowoomba, and south-west past Ipswich.

It takes in major rivers, tributaries, and creeks including the Stanley, Lockyer, Bremer, Oxley, and Warroll, as well as seven dams including Mt Crosby Weir, Lake Manchester, Somerset Dam and Wivenhoe Dam. Brisbane can truly be called a "river city". Within the twenty-six aerial kilometres from Colleges Crossing to Lytton, the river meanders through forty-three suburbs, along a total length of seventy-six kilometres, giving Brisbane 150 kilometres of riverbank from which to appreciate the beauty of this unique waterway.

'Home' (1902-3) Kangaroo Point - was built for John Lamb, co-founder of Edwards and Lamb, a drapery shop which opened in 1879 "at the top end of Queen Street" (their motto), later expanding into a department store. The business survived three wars and two major depressions and remained family owned and managed until sold in 1959.

The mark of a successful man is one that has spent an entire day on the bank of a river without feeling guilty

Chinese Philosopher

discovery

Chapter Two

The history of European discovery and exploration of the Brisbane River is rich enough to match the great adventures of African and American pioneers. But for the fact the main protagonist, John Oxley, was more committed to his calling than scandal, his journeys would feature prominently with Cook, Flinders, and Bass in a rich, heroic Australian pioneering history. Perhaps the early Australian film industry should have documented their deeds and, with poetic licence, enhanced them to legendary proportion as Hollywood has done for Davy Crockett, Daniel Boone, and Dr Livingstone, whose actual exploits may not have been as great or as fearless as our early explorers.

Indeed, the Brisbane River, which is larger than rivers in Sydney and was more suitable for settlement than Melbourne's Yarra, was missed in the detailed expeditions of James Cook and Matthew Flinders. This majestic and beautiful river was protected, its entrance hidden behind the huge sand islands of Moreton Bay, perhaps by nature herself intuitively knowing the abuse soon to be wrought by well-meaning but ignorant European settlers.

The first Europeans to discover the river were shipwrecked former convicts, Thomas Pamphlett, Richard Parsons, and John

"Rhyndarra" (1888-9) Yeronga - built by architect Andrea Stombuco and was until the late 1990s part of an army hospital.

Finnegan. They had set out in a party of four in March 1823 on an expedition south of Sydney to buy cedar, but gales had blown them out to sea and further north than they dared imagine. Having survived the perils of the open sea, and with one of their party dead, the others were saved from inevitable starvation by the Aboriginal population on Bribie Island. It was there Pamphlett was reunited with Europeans when discovered by John Oxley in late November 1823. After rescuing Pamphlett, Oxley searched and found Finnegan and on his second trip a year later found Parsons.

By this stage, Oxley had distinguished himself, rising from a midshipman in the Royal Navy to Surveyor-General of New South Wales in barely a decade. He opened up more farming land, largely along the Lachlan and Murrumbidgee rivers and across the Liverpool Plains, than any previous explorer through his uncharted inland explorations west of the Blue Mountains and as far north as Tamworth. The rivers he charted, flowing away from the coast, led Oxley to be a strong advocate of the theory that Australia had a huge inland sea.

In 1823, Oxley set out from Sydney in the cutter *Mermaid* to examine the suitability for penal settlement at several points along the present-day Queensland coast. This journey

Town Reach - Colonial artist Conrad Martens, who gifted a water colour of the Brisbane River to Charles Darwin, described this as the "prettiest reach of the Brisbane River."

led him to Moreton Bay, where Pamphlett first informed him of the large river they had encountered.

Oxley, aided by Finnegan's directions, made the first planned exploration of the river on December 2, 1823, travelling forty miles upstream to Goodna. The might and majesty of this grand waterway reignited Oxley's belief in and desire to discover an inland sea. He thought this river was the unparalleled tributary required to join such a body of water to the ocean.

Oxley returned to Sydney after a week's exploration, having named the river after then Governor of the Colony of New South Wales, Sir Thomas Brisbane. He returned to the river a year later for a more detailed scientific exploration. Despite seeing much that appealed for a settlement along the river, Oxley recommended a penal colony be established at Moreton Bay. He helped establish penal settlement at Redcliffe in September 1824. The settlement moved to the present site of Brisbane's central business district on the river in May 1825 due to better quality fresh water and few Aborigines, and to problems at Redcliffe including navigational difficulties, troublesome Aborigines, poor soil and timber, and a lack of water.

John Oxley died at Kirkham, his estate near Camden which he had developed for grazing and farming, on May 26, 1828. He was only 45. This midshipman had risen to discover land and waterways untouched by Europeans, providing the base for the settlement expansion that would mark the next century. He has been honoured by towns, waterways, and highways but not yet taken his deserved place in Australian folklore.

"Shafston House" (1851) Kangaroo Point - was originally a small cottage called "Ravenscott" which was altered in 1852 and again in 1883. It has since been used as a residence, kindergarten, nursing home and is now a private education facility.

Former test cricketer Jeff Thomson's boat moored outside entrepreneur James Penny's former home at Hawthorne - a homage to the 1980s.

When you put your hand in a flowing stream, you touch the last that
has gone before and the first of what is still to come.

Leonardo da Vinci

precipitating change

"Carinyah" (circa 1912) Chelmer - built by master plasterer William Bates as his family home.

Throughout this volume, we track the evolution of Brisbane's riverscape during the decades since settlement. But first, it is worth exploring the influences - environmental and social - that shaped development progress and individual residential vernacular. Together with the general economic conditions that influenced residential housing development in Brisbane, riverfront real estate had its own peculiar factors acting to influence its popularity and value.

Brisbane differs markedly from Sydney and Melbourne in that there has been far less grouping of the affluent in particular localities. Melbourne, for example, has whole suburbs of prestige housing, irrespective of any of views or water frontage. Sydney has its harbour, but the eastern and northern suburbs remain popular choices for those aspiring to elite lifestyles and, once again, affluent areas roll from one suburb to another. Brisbane's wealthy are far less centralised and, with the exception of Ascot/Clayfield/Hamilton and some pockets of the western suburbs, quality housing is scattered about Brisbane, positioned in premier hilltop locations rather than particular suburbs.

Bates' plaster work was showcased in his own home.

High and Dry

Brisbane riverfront real estate has now overtaken these hilltops to become the number one status symbol in residential housing, but this was not always the case. The most influential deterrent initially was flooding. Since European settlement, Brisbane has experienced three great floods: in 1844, 1893, and 1974. These, and to some degree smaller floods, were responsible for the "flight for height" mentality. The very early Brisbane settlers, aware of the magnitude of the 1844 flood, started the precedent of selecting hilltop positions to locate their families. Anecdotal evidence suggests that land with both hilltop and spectacular river views was well sought after, but by no means significantly more desirable than other hilltop positions.

The Bulimba Reach retains links to its strong boating heritage.

When Brisbane's growth recommenced after the severe Depression of the 1890s, riverfront real estate was strongly scrutinised, with the disastrous effects of the 1893 flood still fresh in people's minds. The impact of this flood was compounded by the urban growth Brisbane had experienced since Queensland's colonial separation in 1859.

Even when grand homes came down from the hills to riverfront suburbs, the river was still all but ignored. One of Brisbane's premier residential precincts, Laurel Avenue in Chelmer, was subdivided early last century with the attraction of flood-free status and proximity to rail. Many fine homes, even those on riverfront blocks, were built to face the street and made no effort to utilise their river view or facilities. Any premium that did apply to a riverfront location was only established after its elevation and proximity to rail were determined.

In 1927 and 1931, moderate floods occurred as timely reminders of the river's capacity to savage residents. Flood mitigation works, including the commencement of construction of the Somerset Dam in 1935, meant the fear of flooding would slowly dissipate from the community's mind. The Somerset Dam was not completed until 1958 and, by then, other factors were affecting the desirability of riverfront property.

Flooding did occur spasmodically after 1931, and the Brisbane Council's decision to build Somerset Dam seemed vindicated in 1955, when the damage caused by flooding that year was substantially less than in 1893. During these decades, Brisbane's suburban sprawl had continued and began to encroach on the flood plains that authorities believed, through local flood mitigation, were then suitable for residential housing.

During the Australia Day long weekend in January 1974, Cyclone Wanda, which crossed the coast near Fraser Island, degenerated into a rain depression and sat over the Brisbane River catchment area. Some 642 mm (more than 25 inches) fell around Brisbane in 1$\frac{1}{2}$ days. This was on top of the heavier than usual January rain that had already occurred. Somerset Dam became ineffectual, and the water poured down both the Brisbane and Bremer rivers.

Suburbs all over Brisbane, not only riverfront, were inundated as creeks backed up to make

"Tighnabruaich" (1892) Indooroopilly - designed by architect F.D.G. Stanley for his brother H. C. Stanley. Photograph Richard Stringer.

the flooding even worse. Once the banks of the river had been broken, flooding spread across low-lying contours kilometres inland. In some places, the Brisbane River had grown to almost eight times its usual size, and was estimated to be three kilometres wide.

The year 1974 will not be forgotten, as it commenced with the Brisbane floods and natural disaster struck again at the end when Cyclone Tracey devastated Darwin on Christmas Day.

Eighty years of rapid development had taken place since the last great flood. Property, industry and social damage was massive, with approximately 14 000 houses destroyed or damaged in Brisbane city and a further 4 000 in Ipswich. The extensive damage to the central business districts of Queensland's two major cities completed the disaster. The Wivenhoe Dam had already been proposed, and this flood gave impetus to the construction, which was completed in the mid-1980s.

The effects of flooding on riverfront residential development are still remembered by those involved in Brisbane's early property markets. Mr Alan White, former managing director of Ray White Real Estate and son of the founder Ray, recalls the sobering reminders the 1931 floods had for those still concerned by the 1893 disaster. Mr White suggested that then, and now, it takes Brisbane people up to fifteen years to overcome flooding fears. Even with the security of the new Wivenhoe Dam, it wasn't until the 1980s that Brisbane re-embraced riverfront living in areas flooded in 1974.

Industry, not amenity, takes precedence, Peters' 2nd Slip, Kangaroo Point pictured here 1920s. Photograph courtesy of Maritime Museum.

Transformation - lifestyle takes precedence over industry, Dockside, Kangaroo Point pictured here 2003.

Working Waterfront

Floods, though obvious, were not the only factor hindering the initial appeal of riverfront localities. The current city of Brisbane was formed in 1925 when several local councils merged. The new city, then the largest by area in the English speaking world, designed a new municipal emblem encapsulating Brisbane's economic priorities at the time: a steamer approaching land and a lighthouse, grazing livestock, a man with cattle and a shovel, and a ship alongside goods on a wharf. Today, only a sharp eye could spot the remains of Brisbane's wharves, which were both the backbone of its economic development for 150 years and a deterrent to living on the river.

Brisbane city was a working port right up to the 1950s. Wharves lined the northern side of the river at Hamilton and Newstead to New Farm, Petrie Bight to the Botanic Gardens, and right along the current South Bank Parklands. The majority of wharves were built between 1859 and the 1890s, at which time all of Queensland's trading was done via ship transport. Indeed, the rail link to Ipswich was not established until the late 1880s. This working nature of the river hindered the aesthetic benefits for riverfront owners, as well as limiting the amount of land available for residential use.

Peters' Slip and the Evans Deakin workshops at Kangaroo Point pictured here in the 1970s. Between 1940 and the mid-1970s the Evans Deakin Shipyard produced a total of 82 vessels until the demise of Brisbane's major shipbuilder. Photograph copyright The Courier-Mail.

"Dockside", Kangaroo Point - Architect Desmond Brooks designed the visionary "Dockside" concept for Fricker Bros (SA), the winning tenderer for the old Evans Deakin Shipyard. The Dockside Hotel and the Moreton Tower, on the left of the picture, together with their villas and the Town Square, were completed before the recession of the early 1990s and the Stradbroke and MacLeay Towers, on the right, were built by the FA Pidgeon and Sons and the Girdis Group of companies who completed the precinct.

A Hawthorne house (circa 1918) - Federation-style with a colour coordinated boat and shed.

The South Brisbane Dry Dock commenced operation in 1881 and, by this time, Brisbane was a multi-layered city that included secondary industries, port facilities, repair shops, and wharves for dispatching Queensland's rich agricultural produce. At Kangaroo Point, JW Sutton & Co Iron Foundry was, during the 1880s, employing over 350 men building steamships, steel barges, and railway bridges for this booming region. The Brisbane Fish Markets began operations at South Brisbane, in front of where the Queensland Performing Arts Centre now stands, in 1909.

At this stage, the Brisbane River was still clean and unpolluted, and recreational facilities abounded along its banks. These included public baths at the Botanic Gardens, South and East Brisbane, Hawthorne, West End, Dutton Park, and Graceville. The dry dock at South Brisbane was often used for swimming carnivals, including the Barry Cup. Central Brisbane

The view from Lower River Terrace, South Brisbane over the future South Bank Parklands site pictured here around 1890. Photograph courtesy of Maritime Museum.

The Brisbane Milling Company building ("Seafoam Flour") and wharf is at left of picture and Burke's Wharf at right. Burke's wharves and offices adjacent were home to the John Burke Shipping Line, Queensland's only coastal shipping service from Brisbane to Thursday Island. Photograph courtesy of Maritime Museum.

This magnificent inner-city riverfront site was once home to bustling wharves, warehouses, offices and industries is now home to the internationally acclaimed South Bank Parklands.

continued to be a port precinct until the 1940s, when the increasing size of ships ultimately rendered the wharves obsolete. In 1942, during World War II, Brisbane authorities expanded the port facilities at Pinkenba and Hamilton, and this progressive relocation of the working ports continued downstream past Hamilton towards Moreton Bay. The new Port of Brisbane facility commenced construction at Fisherman Islands in 1977, where it continues to operate today, out into the bay. This in turn, allowed the beginning of further significant growth in Brisbane's river residential housing.

The rarely used wharves, which were not removed until the 1970s, 80s and 90s, slowly became increasingly dilapidated. The degenerative impact this had on the central reaches of the Brisbane River and, indeed the whole image of the city, can not be underestimated. Many of the wharves were taken over by other industries, warehouses and carparking, blocking out Brisbane's premier inner city river precincts.

The emergence of the Gold Coast as an exciting city in the 1960s exacerbated Brisbane's struggle with its identity. Instead of being a bustling port, it was a branch office capital, having difficulty reinventing its image. Brisbane, from the 1960s to the 1980s, had become a place to work and sleep, and residents escaped, entertained and holidayed on the Gold Coast. As the State Government Tourist Commission

Architect Harry Seidler's Riverside Centre (1986) was one of the catalysts for waterfront gentrification.

positioned Queensland on the national and international stages as a large beach resort, Brisbane's development of its greatest asset, the river, was impeded. It was the World Trade Fair and Exposition of 1988 that awoke Brisbane from its self-imposed malaise and saw it re-establish itself as a sub-tropical destination in its own right. The staging of "Expo 88" was an initiative of Sir Joh Bjelke-Petersen. Despite some 'doubting Thomases', this major event following Brisbane's successful 1982 Commonwealth Games finally awakened Brisbane to the potential of its riverfront site. Subsequent redevelopment of the Expo site, together with the gentrification of the Eagle Street commercial river precinct, were swift and impressive.

Those redevelopments, and the establishment of the Kangaroo Point Cliffs precinct through a community led initiative, have been catalysts for the rediscovery of residential and commercial riverside real estate. Brisbane today bears few reminders of its time as a working port. Apart from some ship building still in Bulimba, the large ship repair and ship building industries have relocated, together with the wharves, effectively and efficiently towards the river mouth at Moreton Bay.

Ecology Under Siege
Though fewer ships were plying their trade on the river, its fragile environment remained at risk. By the 1920s, the rapid expansion of

"Wolston House" (1852) Wacol - built by William Pettigrew on the junction of Wolston Creek and the Brisbane River. Photograph by Richard Stringer.

the population, now up to 230 000, was placing the eco-system of the Brisbane River under siege. The river was being treated merely as a highway for commerce and, worse still, an outlet for city drainage. In the 1920s only a few of Brisbane's wealthier families had installed septic systems, so earth closets (the backyard dunny) continued to proliferate in most parts of the city. In 1927, a riverside sanitary depot was established near the Victoria Baths, adjacent to the Victoria Bridge, from where sanitary barges carried loads of night-soil downstream, which were dumped into Moreton Bay.

In the 1920s, work finally began on a Brisbane sewerage system, but it had limited reach and was severely strained. There was a serious pollution scare in 1934, when an outbreak of typhoid was linked to oysters gathered only a mile from the main sewerage outfall at Luggage Point. These problems continued right through the 1950s, despite becoming an issue in the 1949 Council elections, affecting not only the perception of our river but the whole city image.

In 1961, night carts were still regularly clearing 80 percent of Brisbane's suburbs, decades behind the progress made in the larger cities of Sydney and Melbourne. It was not until the City Council administration of the 1960s and 1970s, under then Lord Mayor Clem Jones, that most of the city was sewered. Not surprisingly, the long-term practice of disposing of Brisbane's human waste in our waterways adversely affected

Cast iron lace frames the riverside verandah of "Amity" (1892) - the last surviving timber riverfront home at New Farm.

the eco-system of the Brisbane River and Moreton Bay. The sanitary levels of the river, by the 1930s, were so poor that all the riverside baths were closed. This, combined with sediment and mud replacing sandy beaches, effectively rendered the river useless as a recreational facility.

Extracting a Heavy Toll

The condition of this once majestic and clean river was also to be affected by dredging, introducing a further deterrent to riverfront living. In 1865, regular dredging and clearing was introduced to alleviate silt deposits that were limiting the number and size of ships able to use the port facilities. The practice was to continue for more than a century until the new millennium.

Over the ensuing years dredging proceeded to deepen the river bar, lessen the shoals, and provide a channel in the river between Brisbane and Ipswich. Huge work had been done reshaping the river, in particular the Botanic Gardens and the Hamilton revetment wall. Along with dredging came the dumping of the spoil, which also altered the riverscape, intruding right into Moreton Bay, and significantly affected the flow of the river. Salt water once encroaching only to Hamilton now reached past Indooroopilly again altering the natural eco-system. Salt-water mangroves, once not seen past Hamilton, now run sixty kilometres upstream to Jindalee.

"Cremorne" (1905) Hamilton - architects Eaton and Bates. A landmark which cannot go unnoticed when entering Brisbane via the river.

In the late 1880s, it was decided to remove a major obstacle - the rocky bar across the river at Lytton. This was followed by the removal of 1½ acres from the hairpin bend at Kangaroo Point, and more than ten acres were removed from Gardens Point near the Botanic Gardens. Bulimba Point was also trimmed in 1896, and the project completed when Kinellan Point, at New Farm, was cut some years later. This was an infrastructure project of significant size. Over four million tonnes of soil were moved totalling some fifty acres of land. A series of retaining walls, designed to remove the need to dredge navigation channels, was built, along the city, Teneriffe and Hamilton reaches.

Kangaroo Point Cliffs - art on the River Walk creates a vibrant public precinct.

By 1900, the Hamilton wall, over 8 000 feet (about two kms) long, had been finished and work had begun downstream to construct the Doughboy wall. By 1919, when the retaining wall plan was almost complete, more than half a million tonnes of stone for these walls had been removed from the Kangaroo Point quarry helping to create the man made Kangaroo Point cliffs. The massive program of clearing channels and regulating the river flow between rock walls helped to create a modern port, attractive to large steamers, which catered to Queensland's booming agriculture and mineral industries.

Kangaroo Point cliffs, pictured here in the 1970s - still operated as a quarry until 1976. Photograph copyright The Courier-Mail.

As the Brisbane River had long been dredged, the sight in the 1940s of minor sand and gravel dredging created few waves in the community. However, the 1950s and 1960s, with expanding urbanisation and the increasing use of concrete in both commercial and domestic construction, saw dredging grow into a huge extractive industry. These decades were arguably the darkest for the Brisbane River. The concrete industry argued successfully that the river was its most economically competitive source of gravel, a major source of coarse sand, and was vital to the development of South-East Queensland. The State Government actually legislated to assist the industry against the vocal opponents who argued that noise levels and damage to the eco-system were unacceptable.

By the mid-1970s, calls to close down dredging operations became very loud because of the problems of bank instability and noise nuisance to adjacent residents. Slippage along Coronation Drive was stark evidence of the effect of dredging. The amount of sand and gravel being extracted from the river was extraordinary, yet Brisbane's apathy to its river largely continued. Either unaware, or disinterested, the community allowed dredging companies to completely strip the Brisbane River of all its sand, leaving only mud. The noise and bank slippage caused by dredging had a negative effect on the amenity of riverfront living.

The beauty of Brisbane's skyline is mirrored in its river.

These three dark decades saw the continuance of broiler plants in the upper reaches, and abattoirs in the lower reaches, excreting their effluents directly into the river. The resultant effect was the regular sighting of sharks, which ensured those unperturbed by the pollution levels would not enter the water for fear of attack. Two power stations operated on the river, right in the centre of Brisbane at New Farm and Tennyson. The regular ashing from these power stations, of adjoining suburbs, decreased real estate values accordingly. Housewives living nearby had to check the wind direction before hanging out their washing on their Hill's hoists! During these decades, the river was facing its greatest challenges: high pollution levels, decaying ports, no longer appropriate placement of industry, and general public apathy to its plight.

With intense fruit and vegetable farming after World War II came modern farming technologies which, through the use of irrigation, chemical fertilisers and pesticides, were also affecting the river's catchment areas. Heavy rains washed chemical-laden soils into tributaries, and thereafter the Brisbane River, degrading water quality. Industrial waste, including toxic chemicals, increased and more and more inadequately treated sewerage contaminated the river.

Environmental Awakening

The severe flood of 1974 was perhaps the saviour of the Brisbane River. It shocked the Brisbane community, local authorities and

Bulimba Ferry Terminal (1922) - by architect George Addison.

New Farm Ferry Terminal (2003) - by Cox Rayner Architects. Photograph Stefan Jannides.

the State Government, making it obvious that sections of the riverbanks had become dangerously unstable, and management of the river and its tributaries was required. The environmental movement was gaining momentum in the early 1970s, and all levels of government were under greater scrutiny on environmental issues. Relocation of South-East Queensland's electricity generation to huge regional power stations was a positive move, and the government stepped in to regulate dredging in 1975.

By the 1980s, the urgent need to better manage the river was gaining recognition. The Commonwealth Games in 1982 brought Brisbane to the attention of the entire Commonwealth, and the river was highlighted as one of our most important assets. In 1987, Brisbane's then Lord Mayor Sally-Anne Atkinson announced Council's "River City '88" strategy. The single event most responsible for the awakening of Brisbane's conscience over the treatment of its river came with the announcement that the World Fair, Expo 88, would be held in Brisbane as part of the celebrations of Australia's bicentenary. The site chosen for Expo was the previously decrepit wharves which had recently been removed and landscaped, then known as Clem Jones Gardens and the industrial and commercial area at South Brisbane. Brisbane Expo was one of the most successful World Trade Fairs ever held. Brisbane's community embraced it wholeheartedly, thriving in the cosmopolitan ambiance created by pavilions from thirty-five countries. Its riverside location, on the

"Cook Terraces" (circa 1888) Milton - the *Undue Sub-Division of the Land Prevention Act* stopped terrace homes being built in Brisbane. Photograph Richard Stringer.

doorstep of the city's central business district, was the perfect backdrop for international food stalls, beer halls, and entertainment. Nature, as if knowing this was our chance to shine, turned on the best six months of weather Brisbane could offer, and the community basked in the glow of the international praise that was showered upon its city.

Meanwhile, various segments of the splendid new Cultural Centre have been completed on both sides of the southern end of the Victoria Bridge after Expo 88. The public quickly demanded that governments aggressively reclaim the river. The people wanted the outdoor cafe lifestyle, river parks and bikeways it had sampled during Expo. This saw a string of inner-city riverside redevelopments,

"Amity" (1892) Teneriffe - built by Thomas Welsby, the "father" of Queensland rugby union.

which revamped the image of the entire city. These included transforming the Expo site into South Bank Parklands, and the continuing completion of the cultural precinct.

Further along the river, the redevelopment of the Kangaroo Point Cliffs as parkland during the early 1990s provided much wanted public access. Harry Seidler's dramatic design for the Riverside Centre - Brisbane's landmark office tower - had for the first time incorporated general public access to the river. Access quickly expanded right along Eagle Street to the Botanic Gardens. The massive redevelopment of the Evans Deakin shipbuilding complex at Kangaroo Point into the Dockside precinct was quickly followed by the redevelopment of disused wharves and warehouses at Newstead (general cargo and oil), Teneriffe (wool stores), and New Farm (RAN facilities and CSR Sugar Refinery).

"Tintagel" (1986) Tennyson - Business dynamo and lover of Queensland heritage, Ann Garms, created this mansion, recycling materials from various early colonial buildings.

"So-this-is-a-River," said the Mole.

"THE River," corrected the Rat.

"And you really live by the river? What a jolly life!"
"By it and with it, on it and in it," said the Rat. "It's brother and sister to me, and aunts, and company, and food and drink, and (naturally) washing. It's my world, and I don't want any other. What it hasn't got is not worth having, and what it doesn't know is not worth knowing. Lord! The times we've had together."

Kenneth Grahame, The Wind in the Willows

settlement

Along with San Francisco and Istanbul, Brisbane is one of the world's great timber cities. This came about despite the residual fear in the Empire that was the legacy of the 1605 Great Fire of London. Indeed, Brisbane's own disastrous fires destroyed parts of the city in 1864. Melbourne and Sydney adopted regulations controlling building, which were based on British precedents. Brisbane, however, was without controls until the 1864 fires, after which proclamations were issued declaring most of the Brisbane city centre to be "first class areas" requiring external walls of new buildings to be brick, stone, or other non-combustible material. The administration of these provisions proved difficult, and ultimately unsuccessful.

Sitting proudly on Humbug Reach is this striking example of early Queensland architecture.

The majority of heritage houses remaining in Brisbane from those early days of pre-1900 are of brick or stone. These are all examples of what was then elite housing and not representative of the majority of residential developments. Brisbane had an abundance of natural timbers, in particular hoop pine and eucalypt. The advent, in 1853, of steam sawmilling signalled the demise of brick construction for all but the wealthy and, indeed, by the latter part of the 19th century, timber had become acceptable material for all levels of society.

As rapid subdivision was occurring adjacent to town in Petrie Terrace and Spring Hill, effective building regulations were even more necessary and, in 1885, an Act was passed that effectively stopped attached housing, which had been popular in inner suburbs of Sydney and Melbourne.

The *Undue Sub-Division of Land Act* stipulated a minimum lot size of sixteen perches, with a minimum frontage of thirty-three feet. This eliminated the prolification of eight perch lots and established the almost universal pattern of Brisbane houses being detached, and enabled the continued and almost exclusive use of timber for domestic building. A further consequence would be that terraced housing was prevented. However, rules were circumvented, as evidenced by well-known surviving examples such as Cook Terraces in Coronation Drive (page 44), The Mansions in George Street, and The Terraces in Petrie Terrace.

Newstead Wharves pictured here in 1984, home of the US 7th Pacific submarine fleet during World War II. Photograph copyright The Courier-Mail.

"Catalina" (2003) Newstead - transformed by Meridien Developments, architects Fairweather Proberts.

Brisbane's hilly terrain and reactive soils were also vital factors in the preference for timber construction. Architect Richard Suter, who had arrived in 1865, advocated the use of raised floors and stumped houses for both improving ventilation in Brisbane's sub-tropical climate and as a way of countering slopes and reactive soils.

The timber 'Queenslander' was not without its problems and was initially beset by white ant infestation. These constructional shortcomings were remedied by progressive architects with the insertion of ant-capping and the replacement of fireplaces with cast-iron stoves. As much as we would like to claim the 'Queenslander' as our own, it would appear it had been introduced to Brisbane by architects and builders from other tropical colonies, in particular Natal, the Caribbean, and India.

Dilapidated charm - this East Brisbane Queenslander sits high and proud.

The 1880s heritage homes featured in this book are certainly Brisbane's elite of the period. When Brisbane was first being settled, outside the present-day inner commercial districts, ten-acre blocks were the predominant subdivision size of early land grants. Many homes that were originally riverfront have subsequently had their land re-subdivided and may now be several streets back from the water.

Flooding played an important role in the location of housing. John Oxley had noted that a significant flood had occurred between his first and second visits in 1823 and 1824. Settlers who began to build homes after separation from New South Wales in 1859 had the floods of 1841, 1843, and particularly 1844, which was the second significant flood in the short life of the settlement, still fresh in their minds.

Wealthy merchants were naturally drawn to the top of the many hills that offered dramatic views of the river, cool breezes, and safety from rising waters. Surviving historic residences give wonderful testament to the architectural brilliance and building quality of the period. Advances in building technology have only shortened the time taken to construct these grand homes, without being able to improve on their quality.

"Newstead House" (1846) (page 66), overlooking the Brisbane River, at the mouth of Breakfast Creek, is the oldest surviving example of riverfront housing in Brisbane. It is designed and positioned to optimise the scenic view of two reaches of the river. "Bulimba House" (1849-50), on the opposite bank, has since been obscured by surrounding subdivision and can no longer be seen from the river. "Wolston House" (1852) is another early example, overlooking the junction of the Brisbane River with Wolston Creek. These homes were constructed of stone and/or brick, generally with slate roofs. All these homes appear to have had some type of verandah as part of the original construction, although other verandahs have been added at a later date.

Homestead-style on the river, characterised by deep shaded verandahs and dormer windows.

This spectacular early 1900s colonial at Hawthorne has been extended in keeping with its original style.

Prominent heritage homes that retain their links with the river include "Moorlands" and "Cook Terraces" on Coronation Drive, "Shafston House" at Kangaroo Point, "Amity" at Teneriffe, "Rhyndarra" at Yeronga, "Tighnabruaich" at Indooroopilly, "Verney" (now Beth-Eden) at Graceville, and the Lamb residence ('Home') at Kangaroo Point. 'Home' is the only intact building of those named and continuously occupied by descendants of the original owners. The Regatta Hotel has also kept its links to the river, and has been renovated to reinstate the original grand position it held at the turn of the century.

During the 1880s, Brisbane was enjoying a boom period, with traders and then speculators converting their wealth into bricks and mortar. Though not typifying what might be called a Queenslander, these residences nonetheless were individualistic statements by our prosperous early families. These stately homes combined traditional European architectural styles with some tropical pizzazz, more grandiose and flamboyant than what was to follow. In the early 1890s, both economic and physical disaster struck. The disastrous 1893 flood, which caused widespread devastation throughout Brisbane, combined with the economic malaise caused by a national recession, stalled the building of these grand 19th century residences.

Brisbane's early residential development closely followed the railway lines. It is unusual to find grand colonials, pre-dating the advent of the automobile, more than a comfortable walk from a railway station. The best examples of early 20th century Queensland architecture are found nearby these steel tracks, with the finer homes on the hilltop locations. As the Brisbane River meanders through numerous suburbs, departing from the railway lines, development of its foreshores was spasmodic. Large parcels of prime riverside land remained farmland or virgin scrub and were not developed until as late as the 1960s. Though occupying unique, and now desirable and prestigious positions, houses in riverside suburbs generally followed the architectural trends of any given period.

Brisbane's changing seasons - March

- November

- January

Brisbane CityCats, introduced in November 1996, added a sense of excitement to the river.

I have never seen a river that I could not love.

Moving water ... has a fascinating vitality. It has power and grace and associations.
It has a thousand colours and a thousand shapes. Yet it follows laws so definite that
the tiniest streamlet is an exact replica of a great river.

Roderick Haig-Brown

This intricate cast-iron tower fabricated in
Yorkshire in 1912 was erected near this site to
strip tar and ammonia from coal gas produced by
the South Brisbane Gas and Light Company Ltd.

extreme
contrasts

C h a p t e r   F i v e
1 8 0 0 s

Queensland had officially become an independent colony on June 6, 1859, and struggled economically until the 1870s. Indeed, in 1866, Brisbane was plunged into a financial crisis when news arrived of the failure of the Agra and Masterman Bank, financiers for Queensland's railway construction program. Between July and August that year, 156 bankruptcies were recorded, evidence of the prevailing economic conditions.

Gold discoveries in Gympie in 1867, and later in Charters Towers, the Gilbert/Palmer Rivers, and Mount Morgan, powered the Queensland economy into its first long, sustained boom period. The gold rush was supported by a vigorous agricultural industry, in particular sugar along the east coast, and cattle and sheep inland. The fruits of these industries found their way to Brisbane for transportation nationally and internationally.

Queensland enjoyed a sustained twenty-year economic growth period, and it was during this time that most of our significant heritage buildings were constructed, including those that remain proudly on the banks of the Brisbane River.

It is interesting to note that all the grand houses built during this boom period were designed and positioned to optimise their river views and aspect. At this time, the Brisbane River still resembled the "Garden of Eden", with clear water and sandy beaches. Swimming and fishing were popular

Prominent colonial architect Richard Gailey designed the Regatta Hotel, Toowong.

pastimes. The homes featured here are not representative of the average Brisbane home of the time, but are those of successful traders, businessmen, and colonial bureaucrats - commercial and community leaders of the era.

"Newstead House" (page 66), picturesquely situated where Breakfast Creek enters the Brisbane River, enjoys one of the best aspects and river views available in Brisbane. The land was purchased by prominent squatter Patrick Leslie in 1845. He immediately erected a small house in 1846 which he sold in 1847 to captain John Wickham and his sister-in-law, Anna Wickham, who was the grandniece of Captain John Macarthur, "father" of Australia's sheep industry.

"Moorlands" (1892) Auchenflower - this large Victorian residence has a colourful history. Built by John Maxwell it was sold to Mary Mayne in 1878. Her family replaced the original timber residence with the present house. It was bequeathed to University of Queensland in 1940. Photograph Richard Stringer.

"Shafston House" (pages 17 and 65), a stunning gothic revival home modelled on the popular English style at the time, sits high above the Brisbane River with rolling lawns down to the banks. Church of England pioneer Robert Creyke purchased the land in 1851 and sold the home to grazier Louis Hope in 1859. In later life, "Shafston House", purchased by the Commonwealth Government, became a kindergarten training college and then, in 1920, a nursing home for disabled ex-servicemen. In 1988 the property was purchased back from the Government by restaurateur and Bronco's football club co-owner Garry Balkin, who restored the property. It is currently the headquarters and campus of a private education facility.

"Moorlands" (1892) (opposite page) is associated with one of Brisbane's most intriguing families. Indeed, it features in Rosamond Siemon's *Mayne Inheritance*, a best-selling book written about the life and family of Patrick Mayne, a Brisbane butcher in the early colony, who was alleged to have amassed an enviable property portfolio with seed capital from "ill-gotten" gains. Mayne's son, Dr James Mayne, enjoyed a distinguished career, particularly at Royal Brisbane Hospital, and was a prolific philanthropist. A donation to the University of Queensland, enabling the purchase of its current grounds at St Lucia, was among his many generous bequests. "Moorlands" was sold to its current owner, the Methodist Church, in 1971 and is now a recognisable feature in the grounds of the Wesley Hospital.

"Tighnabruaich" (pages 23 and 64) at Indooroopilly, downstream of the Walter Taylor Bridge, was designed by talented and prolific architect F.D.G. Stanley for his brother Henry Charles Stanley, who resided there from its completion in 1892 until 1902. The Stanley brothers made a huge impact on the fledgling colony - F.D.G. by his architecture, which includes the still-standing head office of the National Bank and the General Post Office, both in Queen Street, and the Queensland Club in Alice Street, and H.C. for designing and building about two-thirds of the colony's railways, exceeding 2750 miles of steel. Unfortunately for H.C., "Tighnabruaich", perched high above the river, was the perfect vantage point, from which to watch the 1893 flood wash away his "chef d'oeuvre" the Indooroopilly Rail Bridge. Purchased by the Army in 1945, "Tighnabruaich" was returned to a private residence in 1999.

"Amity" (pages 36 and 45) is the last surviving timber riverfront residence in New Farm and is a great example of the trend to timber that had been gaining acceptance when it was built in 1892. Thomas Welsby, who built "Amity", contributed significantly to commercial and cultural growth of the city. He was the founder of the Engineering Supply Company of Australia and a Director of the Queensland Brewery and the Royal Bank of Queensland. Welsby was a driving force behind rugby union in the colony - the Welsby Cup is named in his honour. He was Patron of the Amateur Fishing Club, co-founder and Commodore of the Royal Queensland Yacht Club, a member of the Queensland Parliament, and founder of the Royal Historical Society. Welsby also published numerous maps and publications on his beloved Moreton Bay. If you look closely at "Amity" from the river, you can see Welsby's personal touches, including garden edges from Moreton Bay coral. One can only imagine the trepidation and, later, the relief he felt when, barely months after the completion of his residence, the 1893 flood stopped just short of his floorboards.

Disaster struck Brisbane both physically and economically in 1893, with the onset of the colony's first great flood. Previous floods had come at times when Brisbane was unsettled,

"Tighnabruaich" architect F.D.G. Stanley's work includes the National Bank and the General Post Office both in Queen Street, and the Queensland Club in Alice Street. Photograph Richard Stringer.

and, for over fifty years, the river had lulled the population into a false sense of security. The river issued two warnings in 1887 and 1890 when flooding occurred, but the community, buoyed by the booming economic times, chose not to heed her warnings.

The 1880s had been a boom decade for Queensland, and belief had spread that the wealth creation and vigorous growth was virtually unstoppable. Inevitably, time proved this incorrect and, in the 1890s, a severe depression replaced the golden years. The huge expansion of public amenities such as railways, tramways, street lighting, telegraphs, and telephones had been financed with borrowed money. Commercially-based prosperity was also illusory, with enormous sums being spent on non-essential civic beautification, and in overdeveloping remote pastoral expansion.

In the early 1890s, the financial bubble burst. Creditors withdrew their funds, and credit became impossible to find. Commercial and industrial development virtually halted, prices rose, and unemployment increased rapidly. Banks crashed, and the entire community was plunged into a depression. The citizens of Brisbane faced stricken circumstances, and families struggled with hardship daily.

In February 1893, the huge flood struck - natural devastation following the economic. This flood was much higher in central Brisbane than the still-memorable and

Ornate "Shafston House" was once owned by Gary Balkin, who pioneered Brisbane River tourism with his Kookaburra Queen paddle steamers. Photography Richard Stringer.

"Newstead House" (1846) - was purchased in 1847 by Captain John Wickham. As Wickham was the Police Magistrate for Moreton Bay region, Newstead House effectively became an unofficial Government House. Photograph Richard Stringer.

devastating 1974 flood. Farmers saw their crops ruined, residents their houses washed away, and businesses lost stock and premises. The general disruption to commerce compounded financial hardship. Business and indeed everyday living were further adversely affected because the mammoth floodwaters had washed away both the Victoria Bridge and the Indooroopilly Rail Bridge, isolating sections of the community and hindering trade.

In terms of total cost, the economic devastation caused by the 1893 flood resulted in far greater losses per capita than those resulting from the 1974 flood. This catastrophe exacerbated the economic problems that were engulfing Australia and Queensland at that time. In May 1893, three months after the floods, eight of Queensland's eleven banks suspended payments and closed.

timeline

1800s

1846	Patrick Leslie built Newstead House.
1850	April 30 - The Bangalore arrived at Brisbane carrying 392 "exiles" (as convicts of a "better" class had become known). This was the last shipment of convicts to the settlement.
1855	February 21 - Walter Hill was appointed Superintendent of the Brisbane Botanical Gardens.
1859	June 6 - An Order-in Council authorised the Separation of the Colony of Queensland from the Colony of New South Wales. Provision was made for a thirty-seven member Parliament with eleven members nominated for the Legislative Council (abolished in Qld in 1922) and twenty-six members elected to the Legislative Assembly.
	September 6 - The Municipality of Brisbane was proclaimed. It had a population of around 5 000 and included North Brisbane, South Brisbane and Kangaroo Point.
	October 11 - The Brisbane Municipal Council was incorporated, with the Council to be elected by male rate payers. It was decided that Brisbane would become the capital of the new Colony.
1860	November 1 - This year saw Charles Tiffin begin building Brisbane's first Government House at Garden Point and the first 'houses on stilts' made their appearance.
1861	September 25 - general and serious flooding in South-East Queensland during much of the year.
1864	April 11 - About a dozen shops in Queen Street were razed by fire.
	December 1 - Fire again ravaged Brisbane, destroying about fifty shops and other businesses in an area bounded by Queen, George, Elizabeth, and Albert Streets. Damage was estimated to be in the range of £100 000 to £150 000, and the incident became known as the 'Great Fire of Brisbane'.
1866	July 10 - Brisbane was plunged into financial crisis when news arrived of the failure of the Agra and Masterman Bank, supplier of finance for Queensland's railway construction program. Between July and August, 156 bankruptcies were recorded.
1873	June - James Venture Mulligan discovered gold on the Palmer River in northern Queensland. The announcement of this find was on September 3, and a dramatic goldrush ensued with over 35 000 diggers heading for the Palmer River over the next three years.
1876	October - Following a further discovery of gold on the Hodgkinson River, settlers began arriving at Trinity Bay. A settlement and port was established, and named Cairns. The first sales of town land were held on February 15 the next year.
1879	January 21 - Thomas McIlwraith became the Premier of Queensland after defeating Douglas's Liberals in the November elections of the previous year. The most stable ministry to this time, the new government was conservative, pro-squatter, and favoured economic development by, and for, large entrepreneurs. It was to last until November 1883.

timeline

1885 August 10 - A horse drawn tramway operated by the Metropolitan Tramway and Investment Company began operations in Brisbane - on six miles of track laid from Woolloongabba to Breakfast Creek.

1887 November - In this year work commenced on the old Courier-Mail building in Brisbane. Innovative architect Richard Gailey incorporated concrete in its brickwork for structural, waterproofing, and fireproofing purposes - one of the earliest instances of this being done.

1889 July 16 - "Cook Terrace" in Coronation Drive was built at a cost of £6 000.

December 20 - The Melbourne-based Premier Permanent Building, Land and Investment Association collapsed. This heralded the end of the "long boom" and the coming general financial depression.

1890 March - Severe flooding occurred in South-East and central Queensland.

1891 January - The financial crisis worsened, especially in Victoria. Within six months twenty-three banks either failed or suspended payment.

1893 January - February - Following a succession of three cyclones in South-East Queensland and northern New South Wales, disastrous flooding began. The Brisbane River rose twice in twenty-two days, destroying both the Victoria Bridge and the Indooroopilly Railway Bridge, inundating the city, and washing three ships into the Botanic Gardens. Damage was estimated to exceed £1 000 000, and eleven lives were lost. City missioner blamed the flooding on the "prevalent desecration of the Sabbath".

May - Eight of Queensland's eleven banks suspended payment and closed. Most eventually reopened after financial reconstruction.

1896 The automobile made its first appearance in Melbourne. Herbert Thomson of Armadale, Melbourne built a successful steam-powered car, The Thomson Steam Car, and Harley Tarrant of Melbourne imported the first petrol-driven automobile, a 4$^{1}/_{2}$ hp Benz.

February 13 - The steam ferry Pearl, conveying passengers across the Brisbane River because the Victoria Bridge had been destroyed, struck the chains of the anchor of the yacht Lucinda and sank. The total death toll is uncertain, but twenty-eight bodies were subsequently recovered.

1897 June 21 - Electric trams commenced operating in Brisbane.

1899 September 22 - Queensland conducted its first referendum on Federation and decided in its favour.

This year Brisbane and Ipswich were connected by telephone, and the popularity of Sandgate as a leisure resort was confirmed with the advent of the railway: in a single day 8 000 people went to swim there, in gender segregated areas.

Designed for serious boaties, the Lough house at Bulimba.

To live by a large river is to
be kept at the heart of things.

John Haines

dawn of the
Queenslander

Chapter Six
1900s

By the 1900s timber was used in most elite homes. This elegant house is on the river at Hawthorne.

The hardships of the 1890s, coupled with a scarcity of credit, ensured residential construction throughout Brisbane and on the Brisbane River was subdued, particularly compared to the booming 1880s. Timber had become the standard building material. The majority of significant homes constructed during this period were one level, timber residences with corrugated iron roofs. These houses were raised on timber stumps to counter reactive soils, capture breezes and mitigate flood damage.

This Yeronga Queenslander (right) was typical of the period. With memories of the devastating 1893 flood still fresh in people's minds, this home was built on a flood-free block and, when originally constructed, did not face the river. In fact, the house was not subsequently turned to capitalise on its riverfront location until after World War II. Over the next sixty years, this home, like many in Brisbane, was developed underneath, and verandahs were filled in for sleepouts or for additional living areas.

Bougainvillea adds tropical colour to the Brisbane River.

A Yeronga Queenslander (circa 1908) - did not face the river when originally constructed.

Federation-style residences, which were a popular nationwide architectural trend, were also favoured in Brisbane. The principal characteristics of this style reflected artistic movements in England and Western Europe that evolved during this period. The grand Federation houses of the southern capitals were brick construction, characterised by tiled roofs and decorative features, such as curved timber details and stained glass windows. However, in Brisbane, typical Federation residences were timber, some omitted fireplaces but still incorporated stumping and high pitched roofs, characteristic of the Queenslander, creating a category unique to sub-tropical Australia. The Indooroopilly home (pages 74, 75 and 76) was typical of this composite genre. It is interesting to note this residence, although well above the flood line, did not take advantage of its river views.

'Home' (cover, pages 12-13) was built for retailer John Lamb and his family who, after weathering the depression of the 1890s, showed faith in the future of Brisbane by commissioning Alexander Brown Wilson to design this classic federation residence. Builder William Anthony finished construction in March 1903. 'Home' is one of Brisbane's most visually significant residential buildings as it is visible from so many parts of Brisbane, highlighting its unique design, materials, and setting. The Queensland heritage citation states that "the residence has landmark quality and makes a strong aesthetic construction to the townscape along the Kangaroo Point Cliffs".

Stained timber and intricate mantelpiece detailing feature in this Federation-style home.

This Indooroopilly house (above, left and page 76) adapted Federation design to suit sub-tropical Queensland.

timeline

1900   July 9 - Queen Victoria gave Royal Assent to the Commonwealth of Australia Constitution Act, a major provision of which was the establishment of the High Court of Australia.

September 17 - Queen Victoria proclaimed that on and after January 1, 1901, the six Australian colonies "shall be united in a Federal Commonwealth under the name of the Commonwealth of Australia".

1901   January 1 - Federation of the Australian colonies came into effect, creating the Commonwealth of Australia.

1902   December 26 - Brisbane, Rockhampton and Townsville were all formally declared as cities.

1905   In this year Queensland granted voting rights to women and permitted them to be admitted to the practice of law within the State. This was also the year in which the State passed workers' compensation legislation for the first time.

Rich timber interiors were common in Federation style homes.

A view down Long Pocket Reach.

We let a river shower its banks with a spirit that invades the people living there, and we protect that river, knowing that without its blessings the people have no source of soul.

Thomas Moore

This decade started well economically for Queensland with agricultural industries performing strongly. Brisbane relished its role as a port city, boasted numerous secondary industries, and basked in its role as State capital. Dark forces were at work throughout Europe and in 1914 a war of unprecedented scale plunged Europe and Britain's Empire, including Australia, into chaos.

The backdrop of war, the effect of severe droughts, and the concomitant imposition of new taxes worked to dampen the community's desire to create lavish domestic architectural statements. Housing styles remained similar to those of previous decades, with timber Queenslander and Federation styles remaining most popular. Although timber was socially acceptable, some people still insisted on the security of brick. 'Home' (1902-3) (cover, pages 12-13) and "Carinyah" (1912) (pages 20 and 21) are interesting examples of this period's individuality.

Built by master plasterer Walter Bates as his own residence, the grandiose style of "Carinyah" allowed him to display premier examples of his work. Bates, originally from England, was commissioned to undertake leading public works including Government House. While the exterior of "Carinyah" was not spectacular for the period, the interior wall and ceiling plasterwork has remained the unique and prominent feature of this residence. With "Carinya" the verandahs again faced away from the Brisbane River to the north-east, and the property is located clear of the 1893 flood level.

cautious restraint

A Hawthorne Federation-style residence (circa 1918).

The Highgate Hill house on page 85 was a typical Brisbane cottage, evidence that any premium for riverfront land was small. Many modest dwellings occupied prime locations, and still do today, albeit often in renovated and extended form. This home incorporated features typical of the era: timber and tin construction with the only ornate inclusions being leadlight feature windows and archways. Built in a flood-free position, here too, river views were not optimised.

The Brisbane Central Business District skyline framed top and bottom by the Gateway Bridge and the William Jolly Bridge.

The Hawthorne Federation-style (pages 28 and 81) house was again typical of the upper-middle class housing being built in Brisbane at the time. Like many homes along this reach of the river, whose owners often included both amateur and professional boat builders, it utilised its position with boat shed and water access. The land on which this house sits was originally purchased from the Colony of New South Wales in February 1855, for the sum of £195.3.9 sterling. Over the next twenty years the land was subdivided and changed hands many times. It is believed Clara Jarrett constructed the home in circa 1918, when two adjoining blocks were combined.

timeline

1911	April 3 - 139 480 people lived in Brisbane.
1914	August 4 - Britain declared war on Germany.
	August 5 - News of Britain's declaration of war on Germany reached Australia. At noon on the same day, the first allied artillery shot in the war was fired from Point Nepean, to prevent the German ship Pfalx from escaping from Port Phillip Bay.
1915	This was a grim year: The State was suffering the effects of drought, news had arrived regarding the heavy casualties inflicted upon the Australian forces at Gallipoli, and taxes were imposed on land, income, entertainment, postage, and business profit. However, Queensland women gained the right to sit in Parliament, the Majestic Theatre opened in Queen Street, and the Central Technical College was established in Brisbane.
1917	Surfers Paradise opened as a holiday resort then known at Elston.
	December 4 - Electric lighting was introduced to South Brisbane.

It is hard to believe that this charming riverfront cottage hidden in the lush sub-tropical foliage is only minutes from the Central Business District.

Hoop Pine sentinels guard this sprawling Poinciana on the Bulimba Reach.

He thought his happiness was complete when, as he meandered aimlessly along, suddenly he stood by the edge of a full-fed river. Never in his life had he seen a river before - this sleek, sinuous, full-bodied animal, chasing and chuckling, gripping things with a gurgle and leaving them with a laugh, to fling itself on fresh playmates that shook themselves free, and were caught and held again. All as a-shake and a-shiver-glints and gleams and sparkles, rustle and swirl, chatter and bubble. The Mole was bewitched, entranced, fascinated. By the side of the river he trotted as one trots, when very small, by the side of a man who holds one spellbound by exciting stories: and when tired at last, he sat on the bank, while the river still chattered on to him, a babbling procession of the best stories in the world, sent from the heart of the earth to be told at last to the insatiable sea.

Kenneth Grahame, Wind in the Willows

escape to affluence

Chapter Eight
1 9 2 0 s

In the 1920s, people embraced hedonism and escapism. The horrors of the Great War were still too fresh and people looked to the creative arts of fashion, art, and dance to escape their grief. This was a time of studied flamboyance, prosperity, art-deco interiors, and jazz. There were widespread, and very visible affluence and hedonism among the wealthy. Yet Brisbane, at the time, still harboured high unemployment, poverty, and deep-rooted economic imbalances.

Large overseas borrowing by the Government provided much needed public utilities. Overseas immigration levels were high, further boosting the demand for building. Commercial life was active, and the birth of consumerism had begun. The popularisation of motor cars, radios, electric radiators, and refrigerators had begun although the majority of households still relied on ice-chests with home deliveries of ice in large blocks, and did not own motor cars until the Holden car was introduced in 1948 after World War II.

"Fairville" (1926) Norman Park - architect Hall and Prentice, builder and original owner G.H. Turner.

After buying the property in the early 1990s John and Jacky Garnsworthy added an oriental flavour to "Fairville".

This period saw the first sustained resurgence of high-quality residential housing since the boom period of the 1880s. The Brisbane River drew its share of the upmarket architectural and building revival. Flood-free, riverside localities in New Farm, Norman Park, East Brisbane, and Toowong were considered prime residential positions. The buoyant mood called for new architecture, and influences from the southern states of Australia and overseas saw the birth of the Californian Bungalow with its wide eaves and shaped brick columns, and the Spanish Mission revival style.

Queensland architects modified the bungalow and Spanish mission homes, presumably due to climatic conditions, and the resultant style and quality was a continuation of the Queensland vernacular. The original US and southern states version of the Bungalow was a single-level, flat-on-the-ground home, predominately of brick structure. Brisbane architects and builders perched the bungalows upon traditional high stumps, and external construction was usually of weatherboards or stucco over chicken wire. These housing styles were the first to reduce the size of verandahs, which had been an inherent feature in early Queensland architecture.

Blanshard house, New Farm - architect Mervin Rylance designed this fashionable Spanish mission style residence.

The 1920s and 1930s produced quality riverside multiple dwellings, above Mazlin Flats (1935) New Farm.

"Cliffside" flats (1935-6) Kangaroo Point - designed by architect R. Martin Wilson whose father, Alexander B. Wilson, designed 'Home' (cover, pages 12-13) 25 metres downstream, 34 years earlier.

By the 1920s, domestic help had generally become a thing of the past, land prices had risen rapidly, and the size of both the dwelling and the land had reduced from previous decades.

The rapid spread of the motor car, which was introduced in Melbourne in 1896, had alleviated the need to be close to railway stations, and architects now had to incorporate wider driveways and car accommodation.

"Fairville" (pages 88 and 89) at Norman Park is a wonderful example of both the California bungalow, and the fruits of a prosperous decade. The land was originally purchased by George Henry Turner, more for its ability to accommodate a tennis court than for the river views that distinguish it.

Turner was a prolific and successful builder, responsible for many Brisbane landmarks including the monastery at St Laurence's Christian Brothers College at South Brisbane, Nazareth House at Wynnum, large sections of the Mater Hospital and classrooms and dormitories at All Hallows' School. He collaborated with other builders on the Redbank Army Barracks and RAAF Barracks at Archerfield. G. H. Turner also constructed the New Farm Powerhouse, where the walls of his building were three metres thick at the base. He died aged 83 in 1970.

Turner commissioned architects Hall and Prentice, a leading architectural firm that was responsible for landmark Brisbane buildings of the period, including the new City Hall and the Tattersalls Club. His home boasted numerous decorative features, including stunning leadlight and stained glass windows, a ballroom, and a night-lit tennis court that caused problems with shipping. Tug pilots would blow the boat's whistle as a signal for Turner to turn the tennis court lights off.

Overlooking terraced gardens, a riverside pool along the Sherwood Reach.

The 1920s also saw many high-quality flats constructed in premier locations particularly around New Farm (page 91). The Art Deco influence of the period is evident. The Graceville (page 95) and Toowong residences (page 99) are excellent examples of the Spanish mission revival, modified to suit the Queensland architectural tradition, and consequently quite different from those built in other cities at this time.

New England cottage-style often featured amber glass, leadlight windows, tall chimneys and deep sloping roofs like this example at Toowong.

1920s - a period of high-quality and fresh architectural design.

timeline

1920   May 31 - Bundaberg-born aviator Herbert John Louis (Bert) Hinkler won acclaim by flying non-stop from London to Turin in nine and a half hours in a tiny Avro Baby aircraft. He had served with the RNAS in World War I, winning a Distinguished Service Medal, and was attempting to fly home to Queensland. Eight years later he succeeded in becoming the first pilot to fly solo from England to Australia, and his aerial exploits were an important factor in ushering in the light plane era of the 1930s.

In this year construction began on the Hall and Prentice-designed Brisbane City Hall.

1921   April 11 - Bert Hinkler flew from Sydney to Bundaberg in eight and a half hours, breaking his own long-distance flying record. He landed his aircraft in a Bundaberg street, and arrived at his home ahead of a telegram he had previously sent warning his mother of his arrival.

Longreach became Australia's first aircraft production centre.

1923   August - James Cavill opened his first hotel on the south coast at Elston.
The establishment was called the Surfers Paradise Hotel, which eventually gave its name to the area.

The City of Brisbane Act was in preparation for incorporating all of the local councils in Brisbane and their essential services under a central authority.

1925   February 21 - The first elections were held for the Greater Brisbane Council. This had been presaged by the passing of the City of Brisbane Act the previous year, which provided for the amalgamation of around twenty municipal areas and the only Australian city to place its entire local government under one authority. Brisbane City Council has the responsibility for water supply, sewerage, city health, power generation, cemeteries, bus and ferry services, and the maintenance of roads, bridges, and paths. Its annual budget exceeds that of the State of Tasmania.

1927   September 10 - Lone Pine Koala Sanctuary was established.

1928   June 9 - Charles Kingsford Smith, Charles Ulm, and Americans Harry Lyon and James Warner landed in the Fokker F VII b-3m Southern Cross at Eagle Farm in Brisbane.

Swain house (1925) Chelmer - a great example of the Californian Bungalow built for the "father" of Queensland forestry.

Rivers know this: there is no hurry, we shall get there some day.

A. A. Milne, Winnie the Pooh

A 1920s Spanish mission style house on the Toowong Reach with ABC satellite dish behind, top right.

hardship &
heartache

Chapter Nine
1 9 3 0 s

Architecture in the 1930s, like so much of our culture, was shaped by the Great Depression, which began in October 1929 with the stock market crash on Wall Street. The roaring '20s had offered a false promise of prosperity. Too much was bought on credit, and borrowed capital had been frequently spent in areas that were not sufficiently productive to repay their cost.

Working Australians were particularly affected and were under considerable financial hardship. Inflation reached record highs: there had been a drop in the real value of wages, and the highest levels of unemployment in the history of the country were recorded. These problems were exacerbated by the huge surge in immigration during the 1920s. Strikes became more common, tensions fuelling widespread ignorance and arrogance, which manifested in marked class distinction, racism, and sectarianism.

Apart from man-made economic woes, Queensland was also beset by a series of natural disasters: cyclones, prolonged drought, the uncontrolled proliferation of prickly pear, and an outbreak of the plague.

The assertion that, for the first time, Brisbane had been divided into the haves and have-nots could be supported by a study of residential housing of the time. However, despite a decade rife with economic upheaval, evictions and soup kitchen lines, the architecture is surprisingly upbeat and distinctive. Many fine homes, including several featured here, were built during a decade characterised by poverty, homelessness, and family breakdown for many.

The New England cottage style favoured elegant enclosed summer rooms over the open verandahs.

A new housing style had emerged during the late 1920s and continued to be popular with the middle class during the 1930s. The New England cottage-style, romantic and rustic, had become fashionable. The St Lucia residence (right, page 101) was designed by Horace Driver, who had returned from New England and designed many similar residences around Clayfield, St Lucia and Toowong.

"Melora", in Archer Street, Toowong (page 105), is a perfect example of this movement. This half-timber cottage-style home with attic bedroom windows appeared plucked out of rural England. The Tennyson home (page 104) features extraordinary porphyry stone retaining walls and fences, extending from the top of the land right to the river bank. Infrastructure of this magnitude on a residential home was made easy thanks to an abundance of cheap labour.

The 1931 flood, however, was again a stark reminder to potential riverside home owners that building only in flood-free locations was a wise decision.

"Stairway" (1932) St Lucia - designed by architect Horace Driver, was the long time home of W.R. Webster, the biscuit manufacturer, and proprietor of the Shingle Inn.

timeline

1930 January 1 - Australian National Airways, owned by Sir Charles Kingsford Smith and Charles Ulm, commenced operations with a flight from Sydney to Brisbane, the inauguration of a regular intercapital air service.

In this year unemployment in Australia had reached nineteen percent.

April 8 - Brisbane City Hall was officially opened.

November 11 - The Queensland National Anzac Memorial, more commonly know as Anzac Square, was dedicated in Brisbane designed by architects Buchanan and Cowper.

1931 February 1-8 - Flooding occurred from Innisfail to Brisbane, following torrential cyclonic rain. In Brisbane, 1 300 homes were inundated and two people were drowned. Moreton Bay was hit by a 6.9 metre storm surge.

1935 This year saw construction of the Story Bridge (originally to be called the Jubilee Bridge) begin, and the opening of the Hornibrook Highway between Sandgate and Redcliffe.

1936 At Indooroopilly the suspension-design road bridge with toll towers was built utilising cables made for the Sydney Harbour Bridge, and opened on February 11.

1939 September 3 - Both Britain and France declare war on Germany.

September 3 - Australia declares war on Germany 45 minutes after Britain had done so.

Queen Street conveyancer, Edgar Tonkin, used recycled porphyry stone in the riverside retaining walls of his Tennyson house (circa 1937).

"Melora" (1938) - at Archer Street dwarfed by the Toowong Village Tower.

Tennyson house - style on a shoestring budget, the aftermath of World War II material shortages.

Sometimes, if you stand on the bottom rail of a bridge and lean over to watch the river slipping slowly away beneath you, you will suddenly know everything there is to be known.

A. A. Milne, Winnie the Pooh

austerity rules

Chapter Ten
1940s

Golden Crows Ash timber, once widely used in Brisbane homes, was by the 1940s becoming scarce, and was used only in special features.

The 1940s was a decade of tumultuous times throughout the world. Australia, one of the few industrialised nations not a battleground in the global conflict of World War II, could not escape its effects. Labour shortages became dire as our brave men and women went off to fight, and food and material shortages resulted as traditional supplies dried up.

The magnitude of World War II created uncertainty and fear among all Australians. With the bulk of Australian troops serving overseas, the nation undefended, and the Japanese forces sweeping through the Pacific, came the first tangible threat to Australian security. We did, however, remain the "lucky country" because, with a few notable exceptions in Darwin and Sydney Harbour, we were spared invasion.

The second half of the decade saw Australia begin the rebuilding process, conscious of the debt it owed to those service personnel who had made the ultimate sacrifice. Taxation increased significantly, but so too did the range of government services, including social services particularly for ex-servicemen and their dependents.

Residential architecture during this period was subdued, inseparably connected to the

Toowong (circa 1940) - this "moderne" style home took advantage of solid rock foundations to build only metres from the waterline.

Naylor house (1942) - Jilba Street, Indooroopilly.

nation's psyche. Towards the end of the 1930s, a new trend in housing had developed: "moderne", streamlined-style houses. This, together with the conventional Queensland tiled hip-roof home and wide overhanging eaves, were the main architectural styles introduced during the 1940s.

A critical shortage of building materials, both during and post-World War II, stifled the size and quality of houses constructed during the period. The Toowong house (pages 108 and 109) was an original "moderne" home, but was extensively refurbished by architect Darby Munro during the 1990s.

The Naylor house at Indooroopilly (opposite page) and the Rae house at Corinda (below) were both products of the material shortage. Even prime land could not attract quality housing, as indicated by the fibro dwelling constructed at King Arthur Terrace, Tennyson (page 106) on premier north-facing, elevated flood-free land. Although it was cleverly designed, these shortages and economic realities ensured the owners abandoned any grand plans.

Richard Cameron of Cameron Brothers, an estate agent in the 1940s, noted that a premium was paid for flood-free river land, but finance and material shortages meant this didn't translate into the buildings.

Rae house (1944) Corinda - material and labour shortages curbed even the most creative architects during World War II.

timeline

1940   July 6 - The Story Bridge over the Brisbane River was opened by the Governor of Queensland, Sir Leslie Wilson.

1941   December 22 - The first American servicemen to arrive in Australia disembarked in Brisbane.

1945   May 7 - Germany surrendered unconditionally to the Allies at Reims in France.

August 14 - Japan surrendered to the Allies, totally demoralised by the effects of the atomic bombardment.

September 2 - World War II officially ended when the Japanese signed surrender documents aboard USS Missouri.

New Farm Powerstation (1926) - designed by architect Roy Rudson Ogg represents a fine example of early 20th century industrial design. It was decommissioned in 1971.

The Ward house at Norman Park takes breakfast views to a new level.

The Story Bridge - Brisbane's most recognisable icon, opened July 6, 1940. Named for John Douglas Story, a senior and influential public servant, its construction was a triumph for local ingenuity.

The face of the river, in time, became a wonderful book ... which told its mind to me without reserve, delivering its most cherished secrets as clearly as if it had uttered them with a voice. And it was not a book to be read once and thrown aside, for it had a new story to tell every day.

Mark Twain

Griffin house (1956) Sherwood - designer-builders Griffin and Knowlman moved away from the centralised square plan to a rectangular plan.

Wartime rationing on common fuels and food stuffs was finally abolished in the early 1950s, as they became more plentiful. There was significant development occurring in industry as new technologies were implemented and the workforce was replenished by the return of servicemen.

Australia enjoyed a reasonable measure of peace and prosperity, and this was reflected in a resurgence of quality architecture in Brisbane. As in the 1920s, new technologies were significant economic boosters, particularly the introduction of television. Melbourne hosting our first Olympic Games allowed Australia to display itself on the international stage, and this resulted in a new self-belief and confidence.

The Brisbane River benefitted from this resurgence in style and building quality, as evident in the featured homes. Cam Griffin, a partner in prolific designer-builders Griffin and Knowlman, built the second of thousands of Griffin and Knowlman homes on a large, tree-studded lot at Sherwood optimising the river aspect and views from the site.

Griffin's home was based on a rectangular plan, rather than the more traditional square, centralised plan, a move that characterised 1950s and 1960s architecture. Large windows and glazed doors admitted winter sunshine, while deep overhanging eaves kept Brisbane's hot summer sun at bay.

Borsht house (1954) Chelmer - designed by architect Kenneth Drewe.

The Rylance house at Fig Tree Pocket, on a large 10 000m² allotment, was purpose-built for this well-known brick manufacturing family. Rolling lawns and gracious gardens were indicative of the invigorated confidence homebuilders of this era enjoyed. This was one of the first homes to be built on land previously flooded, town planners satisfied with the flood-proofing benefits of the new Somerset Dam.

Brisbane City Council, after the construction of Somerset Dam, had predicted flood levels would never again reach those experienced in 1893. This, plus a fading memory of the devastation caused by that flood, saw the threat of flood no longer a deterrent to riverside living. The subdued levels of a 1955 flood only instilled more confidence in the flood mitigation measures. Council hailed the new Somerset Dam a success.

Fig Tree Pocket (circa 1950) - the Rylance family used bricks from their own Dinmore factory for their fashionable acreage residence.

The 1950s also saw new riverfront land being made available through subdivision. Areas at Yeronga, Fairfield, Tennyson, St Lucia, and Chelmer were sold and developed during this and the following decade.

The Kenneth Drewe-designed house at Chelmer (page 118) was the first built at Chelmer along the Indooroopilly Reach, and again showed characteristics of the period: low-pitched roof, glazed doors, and overhanging eaves. Lower ceiling heights resulting from post-war building material shortages became commonplace in housing.

The Graceville house (below and right), designed by architect Theo Thynne, used new building technology developed post-war: timber stumps were now a thing of the past, having been replaced by steel. Low or flat-pitched roofs predominated on new housing during this decade, and recent renovations by the owners have maintained this design feature.

Flat-pitched roofs predominated on new housing during the 1950s.

Designers were now making optimum use of river views.

Views down the Chelmer Reach.

timeline

1950	February 8 - Petrol rationing, introduced as a wartime measure, finally ended.
	June 16 - Butter rationing ended.
	July 3 - Tea rationing ended.
	July 26 - The Federal Government announced that ground troops would be sent to the Korean War.
1951	The bikini swim suit became a controversial topic.
	This was the year in which Brisbane's trolley buses began operating.
1953	July 27 - A cease-fire was declared in Korea and a demilitarised zone created between North and South which is still manned today.
1954	February 3 - HM Queen Elizabeth II, accompanied by HRH Prince Phillip, arrived in Sydney to commence their Australian tour. It was the first occasion a reigning monarch had visited Australia.
1956	November 22 - HRH Prince Phillip officially opened the XVI Olympiad in Melbourne. They were the first Olympic Games to be held in the southern hemisphere.
	May 19 - In Queensland State Election Labor won its eighth successive victory.
1957	It was the year in which Australia's first gold record was awarded to Slim Dusty for his song "A Pub With No Beer", and the long running television program "Pick a Box" began.
	August 3 - With the Labor vote disastrously split, the first non-Labor government in twenty-five years won power. Frank Nicklin became the new Premier of Queensland on August12.
1958	November 15 - Premier, the Honourable G.F.R. Nicklin, officially unveiled the memorial plaque at Somerset Dam.

School girls "Head of the River" 2004 champions, St Aidan's, prepare to go through their paces on the St Lucia reach. Photograph Mark Elliott.

Keep on rollin' along
Old Man River don't stop your way.
Keep on runnin' from the north, the south, the east or west,
You gotta roll it!

Oscar Hammerstein II and Jerome Kern

modern
daring

Architect Maurice Hearst won acclaim for the Davies house (1966) Fig Tree Pocket.

The advent of the contraceptive pill gave birth, if you will, to the sexual revolution and, with it, extreme women's fashions, particularly the miniskirt and see-through blouses. Cinema and Hollywood's influence was profound and the new wave of music attained heights of popularity undreamt of previously.

Australian bands were at the forefront of the international music scene, with the Easybeats, the Seekers, and singer Johnny O'Keefe. War reared its ugly face again late in the decade with the escalation of the Vietnam War, which was spilling over into neighbouring nations such as Laos and Cambodia. Technological advances continued to drive world economies. The staggering speed of that technology, from the advent of the first satellite to Neil Armstrong's small step onto the moon, in barely a decade, drove advances in international communication and travel.

The 1960s were also a period of great social change in Australia, and women's issues - including uniform divorce laws, equal pay and the legalisation of abortion - had come to the forefront. In 1969, Queensland, largely more conservative than the rest of the nation, chose Joh Bjelke-Petersen as Premier. He was to hold office and shape Queensland policy for the next seventeen years. Decimal currency and postcodes were introduced and, despite a credit squeeze in 1960 and again in the latter part of the decade, the 1960s were a time of growth and prosperity for Australia.

A traveller's palm shields this early 1960s house at Norman Park.

Employment was high, industry was growing, and the economy was generally buoyant. Significant discoveries of oil, natural gases, and enormous reserves of iron ore, bauxite, and nickel had sparked the mineral boom, which raised great economic expectations. Economic and social confidence was reflected, again, in Brisbane's architecture with radical new designs pushing the architectural parameters.

Prominent Brisbane architects Robin Gibson and John Dalton further popularised flat roofs with deep facias and heavily glazed northern aspects. Robin Gibson commenced private practice in Brisbane in 1957 and went

Mocatta house (1966) Yeronga - above and right - architect Robin Gibson. Photograph by Richard Stringer.

Architect Robin Gibson went on to design major public buildings including the Queensland Art Gallery, Museum, State Library, the Performing Arts Centre, and Mayne Hall at the University of Queensland. Photograph by Richard Stringer.

This St Lucia house was a result of further subdivision during the 1960s which took advantage of riparian relaxations.

Northern sun is filtered by jacarandas and large overhanging eaves.

on to be regarded as one of Queensland's outstanding architects. His work included the Queensland Cultural Centre at South Bank comprising the Queensland Art Gallery and museum together with the State Library and the Queensland Performing Arts Centre with its several theatres. He also designed several riverfront residences, including his own home on the banks of the river at Yeronga.

Maurice Hearst won architectural acclaim for the Davies house at Fig Tree Pocket (page 126), which blended into the natural bushland, optimising its elevation and river aspect. Features, including the flat roof made popular in the previous decade, were combined with shapes and daring angles, most distinctively in the lounge.

It was during the 1960s that the Brisbane City Council tightened its riparian setback by-laws, after a court battle with George Mocatta saw him set his Robin Gibson-designed "Queensland House of the Year" just ten metres from the high-water mark. Several other residences, including the St Lucia home (left and opposite page) built in the 1960s, and significantly renovated in the 1990s, were also within the twenty metre setback.

timeline

1960   In this year Sir Frank Macfarlane Burnett shared the Nobel Prize for Medicine for his work on acquired immunological tolerance, Australians won several gold medals at the XVII Olympiad in Rome, Rolf Harris recorded "Tie Me Kangaroo Down Sport" and Aborigines became eligible for social service benefits.

1961   During this year the population of Brisbane had risen to forty-one percent of the State's total.

1963   February 18 - HM Queen Elizabeth II, accompanied by HRH Prince Phillip, arrived in Australia to visit all States and to attend Canberra's jubilee celebrations.

1964   The Beatles toured Australia, Donald Campbell set world land and water speed records at Lake Eyre and Lake Dumbleyung, and Dame Margot Fonteyn and Rudolf Nureyev danced with the Australian Ballet. Australians performed creditably at the XVIII Olympiad in Tokyo, and 'Midge' Farrelly won the inaugural world surfing title hosted at Manly in New South Wales.

1965   This year saw Ampol open the first Australian owned refinery at Lytton.

        Two women chained themselves to the public bar at the Regatta Hotel in Brisbane in an attempt to gain equal access for women. Both worked as lecturers at the University of Queensland, St Lucia, and one is now more famous as actor Sigrid Thornton's mother, Merle.

1966   February 14 - Australia introduced decimal currency to replace the British system of pounds, shillings and pence.

        In this year meter maids were introduced on the Gold Coast.

1968   May - The Australian stock exchanges experienced a boom in mineral stocks.

        June 21 - An official announcement foreshadowed the closure of Brisbane's tramway system by Lord Mayor Clem Jones.

        August 8 - Joh Bjelke-Petersen replaced Gordon Chalk as Premier of Queensland. Chalk was Acting Premier after the death of Jack Pizzey, following the retirement of Frank Nicklin.

1969   July 20 - American astronauts Neil Armstrong and Edwin Aldrin became the first men to land and walk on the moon's surface. They returned safely to earth with numerous pictures taken there together with samples of rock.

        March 17 - Brisbane became the first Australian capital city to receive a natural gas supply when the Roma-Brisbane gas pipeline opened.

        April 13 - The last of Brisbane's trams ran down Queen Street, escorted by police as a precaution against possible demonstrations by the pro-tram lobby.

1960s homes with good proportion lend themselves to refurbishment as seen with this makeover by architect Cox Rayner.
Photograph Mark Burgin.

Revered boat builder Norman Wright moved his business from Newstead to Bulimba in 1935. Three years later "Taree", a Norman Wright 18 foot skiff, won the world championship.

But I remember us riding in my brother's car

Her body tan and wet down at the reservoir.

At night on them banks I'd lie awake

And pull her close just to feel each breath she'd take.

Now those memories come back to haunt me,

They haunt me like a curse,

Is a dream a lie if it don't come true?

Or is it something worse

That sends me down to the river?

Bruce Springsteen

Social reform was perhaps the highlight of Australia in the 1970s. Charismatic reformist leader Gough Whitlam led the Australian Labor Party to a federal election victory in 1972, for the first time in twenty-three years. It was seen as "its time" for a change and there was also community distrust and suspicion of the Liberal Party regarding uranium mining and conscription for Vietnam. Whitlam, however, was controversially dismissed less than three years later, and the Liberals, riding on a platform of economic management, swept back into power in a landslide election.

climate to respect

Chapter Thirteen
1970s

Flat roof design continued into the 1970s.

Porter house (1979) Kenmore - designed by architect Tom McKerrell.

Australia's mineral resources continued to fuel our prosperity and the 1970s saw the development of the Bass Strait Oil Fields and discoveries of natural gas on the north-west shelf and a major diamond deposit in the Kimberley region. Social reforms were afoot, including the lowering of the 'age of majority' to eighteen years, national health care in the form of Medibank, adoption of the Celsius temperature scale, an overhaul of laws in relation to divorce and other family matters, changing of the national anthem, the introduction

Dalton once wrote, "the architect's social responsibility is to the future".

of colour televisions, legal casinos, nude bathing, and the new easy availability of consumer credit through the provision of Bankcard, the first real Australian credit card.

The decade's defining event in Brisbane occurred in 1974, again reminding us of the river's unpredictability. In late January, Cyclone Wanda crossed the coast near Fraser Island and degenerated into a rain depression, sitting over the Stanley and Brisbane River catchments. Some 642 mm (more than 25 inches) of rain fell on Brisbane in just over thirty-six hours. Somerset Dam held some water back, but offered little protection to the Brisbane and Bremer Rivers. As indicated earlier, the massive development seen in Brisbane since the last great flood had devastating consequences, not only for riverfront residences, but for numerous suburbs affected as the river burst its banks and flooded into previous alluvial plains now filled with residential housing.

This event again dampened the value of the riverfront, and made buyers sceptical of flood-prone positions. However, above the flood line attracted new homes and inspired some innovative designs.

In the 1970s, prominent Queensland architect John Dalton was perhaps at the zenith of his acclaimed career, having furthered his reputation after winning the Royal Australian Institute of Architects Queensland Resident "House of the Year" in 1964 and again in 1967.

Musgrave house (1970) Chelmer - designed by architect John Dalton.

Architect Robin Spencer's innovative narrow lot solution.

Dalton could be credited with the return of the verandah to modern Brisbane homes. The Musgrave home at Chelmer (pages 138 and 139) is a good example as he paid particular attention to climatic functioning through adequate ventilation and cooling in this new breed of sub-tropical home.

With timberwork expressed and finished in dark umber stain, a new, highly identified house style had emerged. During the 1970s, there was also a return to the use of trellis screening and simple window shades on eastern and western facades. Roofs, however, followed the farm-shed form rather than the hipped-roof form of the typical Queenslander.

The Tom McKerrell-designed Porter house at Kenmore (page 137) took a more traditional Georgian influence, and was a prime example of a proliferation of grand residences being built in Brisbane's affluent western suburbs. Though large, this house had not yet approached the flamboyant styles Brisbane would soon see in the halcyon 1980s.

The Chelmer house (page 136) displays several features of the decade, including the flat roof, which is typical of the Robin Gibson and early John Dalton designs that were becoming the future models for Queensland architecture.

The Walter Taylor Bridge (1936) (above and top) - which he both deigned and constructed. Walter Taylor was an inventor and an expert on reinforced concrete construction.

timeline

1973   January - The Captain Cook Bridge and the first section of the Riverside Expressway, all made of pre-cast, pre-stressed, box girder concrete sections, off-site, were officially opened after completion late in the previous year.

November 4 - About 600 Brisbane homes were damaged by a tornado which swept through the south-western suburbs.

1974   January - The worst floods since 1893 hit Brisbane following cyclone Wanda. In thirty-six hours some 642 mm (more than 25 inches) of rain fell, inundating roughly a third of the city and partially or totally flooding about 7 000 homes. Twelve people were drowned and around 9 000 rendered homeless. In Ipswich, about 40 homes were swept away. Flood damage was in the order of $200 million. The north-east of the State also suffered severe flooding and large cattle losses were recorded.

1975   March 1 - Colour television was officially introduced, although a few cartoons and sporting events had been televised in colour the previous day.

1976   March 17 - Without prior Cabinet approval, Premier Joh Bjelke-Petersen announced that death duties would be abolished in the September budget, thus precipitating a parliamentary row between coalition members.

In this year preparations were made for the construction of the Queensland Cultural Centre on the south bank of the Brisbane River, and connection of the northern and southern railway systems, via a new Merivale Rail Bridge, commenced. The cross river rail-link was completed in November 1978.

The new Brisbane Botanic Gardens at Mt Coot-tha were officially opened.

1977   January 1 - State death duties were abolished, and over the ensuing years, many retirees from interstate began settling in Queensland.

September 4 - Premier Joh Bjelke-Petersen announced the removal of the right of appeal to magistrates after applications for permits to hold street marches had been rejected.

November 12 - In Queensland State Election, the Bjelke-Petersen National Party Government was returned to office with a majority vote.

December 3 - Brisbane police made over 200 arrests when civil liberties demonstrators protested against street march restrictions.

1979   July 1 - Commonwealth estate and gift duties were abolished following Queensland's decision which was a defining event for Australia's populace.

April - The historically interesting Bellevue Hotel in Brisbane, which had been built in 1886 and had served as a hotel until it was purchased by the State Government in 1967, was demolished.

Moon river, wider than a mile

I'm crossing you in style someday.

Oh dream maker, you heart breaker

Wherever you're going, I'm going your way.

Two drifters, off to see the world

There's such a lot of world to see.

We're after the same rainbow's end

Waiting round the bend, My Huckleberry friend

Moon river and me.

Johnny Mercer

Entrepreneur Keith Lloyd's ability to turn dreams into reality resulted in this Georgian classic at Norman Park.

Cross house (1988) Norman Park - designed by architect Jurgon Buchonea.

opulent &
ostentatious

The 1980s were a particularly colourful decade in Australia's history. Alan Bond, still then a revered figure of Australian business, wrested the America's Cup from the United States for the first time ever and, four years later, the fabled yacht race was held in Fremantle.

The Labor Party won federal office in 1983 with Bob Hawke as Prime Minister and Paul Keating as his Treasurer. Keating deregulated banking and allowed the Australian dollar to float freely on international markets.

Joh Bjelke-Petersen had the Queensland economy firing through rich mineral developments, and his pro-development attitude. Queensland had a 'can-do' attitude and was booming through major taxation initiatives such as the abolition of death duties in the late 1970s. Brisbane began to realise its potential as a leading world city, first successfully hosting the Commonwealth Games in 1982 and then the International Exposition in 1988. Queensland's economy was strong, and the real estate market boomed immediately after the collapse of the share market in 1987.

The opulent '80s saw the rebirth of the grand home, which had been largely absent since the boom years of the 1880s a century earlier. Keith Lloyd's riverside mansion at Norman Park (pages 144-145) set the pace with the new style of grand home and was followed by flamboyant entrepreneur James Penny's Hawthorne home (page 18), Christopher and Pixie Skase's Hamilton mansion, and the Darby Munro-designed Dalglish house at Mactier Street, Fig Tree Pocket (page149).

Architect Jurgon Buchonea designed the distinctive timber residence for Cindy Cross at Norman Park (opposite page and below), which was shrouded in mystery, as little was known of this self-made business woman who had emigrated from New Zealand.

The Wivenhoe Dam was completed in 1985, and promised to reduce the effects of a "one-in-a-hundred-year" flood by three metres. This, plus the fading memory of the 1974 flood, saw the differential between the prices of previously flooded and non-flooded properties close. The premium for absolute riverfront homes began to rise.

Nordic inspired architectural character.

timeline

Burns house (1982)
Fig Tree Pocket - designed
by Andrew Wiley from
Agenti Architects.

1980	Work began on the Gateway Bridge.
1982	June 21 - The Queensland Art Gallery within the Queensland Cultural Centre was opened. Costs had blown out from the original estimate of $10 million to $28 million.
	October 1-9 - Brisbane hosted the XII Commonwealth Games. The event was officially opened by HRH Prince Phillip and officially closed by HM Queen Elizabeth II. Australia won gold medals in thirty-nine events.
	November - The Cloudland Ballroom in Bowen Hills was sadly demolished.
	Lord Mayor Roy Harvey opened the City Mall in Queen Street.
1983	September - Alan Bond's yacht *Australia II*, with a revolutionary winged keel designed by Ben Lexen, beat the American boat *Liberty* to win the America's Cup. It was the first time in the Cup's 132-year history the trophy had been wrested from the New York Yacht Club.
	May 3 - All of Queensland was declared a disaster area after a fortnight of almost continuous rain broke a drought and flooded nine river systems. Rain that began in May continued into the following year, and floods affected not just Queensland, but also New South Wales, South Australia and the Northern Territory.
1985	March 30 - In Brisbane City Council Election, Alderman Sallyanne Atkinson was elected as Brisbane's first female Lord Mayor.
	October 18 - The Wivenhoe Dam was officially opened by the Premier, Sir Joh Beljke-Petersen.
1986	January 11 - Gateway Bridge at 1 027 metres (1.6 kilometres including approach sections), the world's longest cantilevered box-girder bridge, was opened. Throngs of pedestrians and roller-skaters began crossing the mist-shrouded structure early in the morning; Premier Sir Joh Bjelke-Petersen officially opened it at 10.30am. About one in five Brisbanites are estimated to have "walked the bridge" before traffic flowed into the next era of our river crossings.
1987	October 19 - In line with the worldwide stock market plunges, share values on the Australian stock exchanges plummeted in record fall.
	December 1 - Sir Joh Bjelke-Petersen resigned as Premier of Queensland, and was succeeded by Mike Ahern. Sir Joh had spent forty years in politics and his term as Premier - nineteen years, three months and twenty-three days - set a new record.
1988	October 30 - Expo 88 closed with a gala party which included a fireworks spectacular, laser light show, entertainment, singing, and a flyover by RAAF jets. After opening in April 1988, Expo attracted 18 560 000 visits, making it one of the most successful specialised expositions ever held.
1989	December 2 - In Queensland State Elections, the ruling National Party suffered defeat and the Labor Party swept to victory after thirty-two years in Opposition. Wayne Goss became the new Premier of Queensland.

Dalglish house (1998) Fig Tree Pocket - designed by Denham and Munro Architects. This prominent residence incorporated a large pool, stables, and dressage arena. Photographs Damiano Visocnik.

Grand Queensland architecture on the Canoe Reach overlooking Sir John Chandler Park - a spectacular heritage reincarnation at Yeronga (1987).

It was kind of solemn, drifting down the big still river, laying on our backs looking up at the stars, and we didn't even feel like talking loud, and it wasn't often that we laughed, only a little kind of low chuckle.

Mark Twain

embracing river quality

Chapter Fifteen
1990s

Holman house (1995-6) Chelmer - designed by architect Noel Robinson.

The 1990s began a decade of stagnation for the Brisbane real estate market. In the aftermath of the Fitzgerald inquiry, the Goss Labor government was elected with a comfortable majority. In the early 1990s, this was reduced, and in 1995, voters reinstated the National-Liberal Party Coalition with a narrow majority. After a by-election in 1996, the Parliamentary outcomes hung on the decision of a single independent, who chose to support the Coalition.

Mediterranean influence interfaced with sub-tropical design features.

Architect Margie Ward's modern take on the Queenslander at Norman Park.

Views across Humbug Reach, New Farm to the city.

This political instability, coupled with low economic activity, Native Title issues for the mining industry, and droughts for farmers, worked to stagnate growth in Queensland. Unemployment was the highest in mainland Australia, and Queensland did not benefit from the financial services and communication boom experienced in the southern capitals. Alan Bond had already self-destructed, and "business tycoon" Christopher Skase fled the country after being declared bankrupt owing $172 million.

Following the huge surge in housing prices from 1988 to 1991, Brisbane was to experience negative real estate price growth in real terms for the first time since the Great Depression of the 1930s. Little significant housing was produced in the early part of the decade. Nevertheless, the 1990s can be identified as the period during which riverfront real estate assumed its position at the top of the prestige property ladder. Brisbane had, by now, enthusiastically embraced its 'River City' image.

Appreciation of the river had been growing rapidly since Expo 88, with the redevelopment of the Eagle Street Wharves precinct and of the Expo site, the cultural precinct, and the Kangaroo Point cliffs. Brisbane City Council had celebrated 1987 as the 'Year of the River' and, during the 1990s, the river had re-established itself as the recreational and spiritual soul of the Brisbane community.

Heiner house (1999-2000) Indooroopilly - designed by Andrea Heiner, built by Graham Stone was distinctly influenced by modern Mediterranean villas.

International architecture modified to Brisbane's climate.

Homes built during this decade may not have displayed the size and opulence of those that emerged during the 1980s, but many will argue they bear greater architectural merit. The Bulimba residence (page 159), designed by architects Brand and Slater and styled on federation homes, remains uniquely Queensland and pays tribute to the area's architectural history. Indeed, the owners are linked to legendary boat-builder Norman W Wright and the company that bears his name, and their home is three doors down from Wright's original home and boatyard (page 134-135).

The Noel Robinson-designed Holman house at Chelmer (pages152 and 153) was an excellent example of the quality of architecture now being built on the river. Its Mediterranean influence is interfaced with sub-tropical design features to produce both a practical and visually stunning home.

The Baldwin house (page 158) is a further example of grand 1990s riverfront property, indicative of how elegance and functionality had replaced the excess, flamboyance, and brashness of the 1980s.

timeline

1990   January 18 - A spectacularly fierce fire destroyed the old MacTaggart's Wool Store at New Farm. The blaze could be seen from many parts of Brisbane, and in some areas crowds of spectators gathered. More than 20 fire brigade units battled the blaze, but the building was destroyed.

July 7 - The 50th birthday of the Story Bridge was celebrated in style by crowds of Brisbane residents over a "long" weekend.

November - Work began on the reconstruction of the former Expo 88 site on the banks of the Brisbane River. Six cranes and about 100 men began digging trenches for a boat canal, swimming lagoon, and waterways. Other plans for the site at the time also featured parklands, a promenade, restaurants, an aquarium, butterfly house and Gwondana Land Zoo.

"Whistler" (1990) Baldwin house, Yeronga - designed by architect Phillip Grause.

timeline

1991 March 23 - In Brisbane City Council Election, Lord Mayor, Alderman Sallyanne Atkinson, conceded defeat after a very closely fought election. The Lord Mayor-elect was former priest Mr Jim Soorley, who assumed office after the Declaration of the Poll result on April 13.

June 14 - Business "tycoon" Christopher Skase, called to account for debts of $172 million, was declared bankrupt and was banned from leaving the country. After surrendering his passport, Skase successfully reapplied for it, and flew out of Australia less than 24 hours later, never to return.

1992 March - The Brisbane Bears AFL team move their home ground matches to the Gabba. It would take ten seasons, and a merger with the Fitzroy Lions from Melbourne, until the team's first premiership in 2001.

June 20 - Sir Walter Campbell, Governor of Queensland, declared South Bank officially opened. Attracting more than eight million visitors every year, this 17 hectare redevelopment of the Expo 88 site has become a landmark and central meeting point for Brisbane's residents and tourists alike. Encompassing the Performing Arts precinct, Gallery, Museum, and Library - all overlooking the river - South Bank is also home to the only inner city beach in Australia.

1993 It was in this year that Personal Investor Magazine declared Brisbane "Australia's Most Livable City". The rejuvenated river, and riverfront lifestyle, was a key factor in the decision.

1995 July - Brisbane moved to eight digit phone numbers, with residents reminded to add '3' to their phone numbers, and the rationalisation of national area codes brought Queensland closer together.

1996 February 20 - A tight Queensland State Election resulted in a 'hung' parliament, with Independent member Liz Cunningham holding the balance of power. After some deliberation she announced her support for the National-Liberal coalition, and Rob Borbidge is sworn in as Premier.

November - The final catamaran of the first stage of CityCat ferries was launched. Servicing the Brisbane River from Brett's Wharf, near the Gateway Bridge, to the University of Queensland, six CityCats were launched progressively in 1996 to augment the slower traditional-style ferry services.

1997 September - Brisbane celebrated its first annual River Festival, which has since grown to be one of Brisbane's iconic events, attracting tens of thousands of people every year for a celebration of the river, with events such as River Fire and River Symposium.

1998 June 26 - A second tight Queensland State Election resulting in another "hung" Parliament, this time with Independent member Peter Wellington left with the casting vote. Deliberation again before he announced his support for Peter Beattie, so the Labor Party returned to power. With the declining One Nation Party vote before the State elections in 2001 and 2004, Beattie, the self-titled "media tart", gained a large majority in the Parliament.

Wright house (1995) Bulimba - designed by Brand and Slater Architects.

"Believe me, my young friend, there is NOTHING - absolute nothing-half so much worth doing as simply messing about in boats. Simply messing," he went on dreamily: "messing-about-in-boats: messing-"

Kenneth Grahame, Wind in the Willows

The new millennium signalled a new beginning for the Brisbane residential property market, introducing positive growth for the first time in ten years. This was to accelerate into a real estate boom during the next four years. Australia, with the exception of Sydney, had missed the northern hemisphere growth surge experienced in the mid-to-late 1990s, but consequently also missed the economic downturn experienced by our northern neighbours after the dot-com meltdown.

premium position

Chapter Sixteen
2000s

Fig Tree Pocket - constructed by Osterfield and Johnson, this 2000m² home set a record price for Brisbane's residential homes when sold in 2003.

Michael Rayner of Cox Rayner Architects used stainless steel, zinc, and natural stone to set a new bench mark with this St Lucia house (2000). Photograph Mark Burgin.

Riverfront real estate had established itself as the number one prestige residential position. More million dollar-plus sales had occurred along the river than in any other locality or region. Brisbane had taken the river to its heart, and the upwardly mobile wanted to live on it. Continuing residential and recreational renewal along the riverbanks, the cessation of dredging, and the relocation of redundant industries all contributed to boost the city's river pride.

A sea-change was happening Australia-wide, and Brisbane people were once again viewing their river for the waterway marvel that it is. In 2002 the Brisbane City Council introduced the "Brisbane River Management Scheme", giving residential riverfront real estate its own local plan and further recognising the uniqueness of this position.

Distinctive entry to this St Lucia house, the architects Cox Rayner Architects also designed Brisbane's Goodwill Bridge on the South Brisbane Reach. Photograph Mark Burgin.

Architectural standards continue to set new benchmarks as owners strive to capitalise on the escalating premiums paid for riverfront land. Architect Michael Rayner's design at St Lucia (opposite page and above) is a premier example: building the home over the top of the existing residence to optimise its unique position inside the riparian regulation line. Rayner's use of stainless steel, zinc, and natural stone has set new architectural standards.

Architect Margie Ward's treatment of a vacant site at Norman Park (pages 113, 154 and 155) displays the thought and consideration architects were giving to their immediate environment. Traditional, early-century Queensland architecture was modernised to optimise the views, aspect, and riparian facilities available from the site.

Catalina, Newstead - the first stage (completed in 2002) of nine homes and four units was designed by MPS Architects. The second stage of nine houses and three units by Fairweather Proberts was completed in 2003. Photograph Shane Holzberger.

Views across the Bulimba Reach to Hawthorne. Photograph Shane Holzberger.

Progressive design and fresh building materials were a hallmark of Meridien Development projects. Photograph John Linkins.

The Doran residence at the Brisbane Corso, Fairfield (below and right) utilises elements drawn from our tropical Balinese neighbours to create a unique design. Architects Hanniford and Knight have blended the owner's interpretation of this increasingly popular style, incorporating grand gardens and comfortable outdoor living areas with the functionality expected of modern homes. Remnants of the river's history have also been maintained, with the original jetty and boatshed retained to add yet another dimension to a unique lifestyle residence.

The Doran house (2002) Fairfield (above and right) - designed by architects, Hanniford and Knight incorporates Balinese gardens and outdoor living areas.

The Heiner house in Indooroopilly (pages 156 and 157) is a further example of riverfront owners seeking unique lifestyle residences. Distinctively influenced by modern Mediterranean villas, it is also an example of recent international architectural trends, modified into a uniquely Queensland style that better suits this climate and lifestyle. Unlike those styles imported during the 1920s, this residence embraces the river aspect it enjoys, positioning the main living areas and the pool to overlook this majestic reach of the river.

timeline

2000   September 13-23 - Brisbane's Gabba ground hosted six preliminary games and one quarter final soccer match as part of the Sydney Olympic Games. Despite a lack of local teams, Brisbane supported the matches with average crowds averaging above 30 000 people.

2001   May 6 - Suncorp Stadium (Lang Park) hosted its last match before a $280 million redevelopment commenced. A sell-out crowd watched Queensland thrash New South Wales 34-16 in a memorable State of Origin match that night, amidst great controversy about the Lang Park decision compared to a site at the R.N.A. Showground (The Ekka).

August 6 - Christopher Skase, still wanted for his company's debts totalling $172 million, died in Spain where he avoided questioning for more than ten years.

August 28 - September 9 - Brisbane again proved its ability to host a major world sporting event when it hosted the Goodwill Games.

October 21 - Queensland Premier, Peter Beattie, officially opened the Goodwill Bridge.

2003   May - After twelve years as Brisbane's Lord Mayor, Jim Soorley resigns.

June 1 - Almost two years of redevelopment work were completed at Suncorp Stadium, which was relaunched as a world-standard sporting venue. In its first months it played host to rugby league State of Origin matches, and several games as part of the 2003 Rugby Union World Cup.

2004   February 7 - In Queensland State Election, Beattie Labor Government returned still holding a large majority vote.

March 27 - In this year's Council Election, Brisbane chose Campbell Newman as the new Liberal Lord Mayor over the unelected incumbent Tim Quinn.

August 27- September 5 - River Festival 2004 opened for an event-packed fortnight. The highlight again was River Fire and organisers extended the riverbank viewing positions with fireworks focal points extending from Coronation Drive to the Story Bridge. Hundreds of thousands of people again thronged to the event, still centred on South Bank, and two F111s thrilled the crowds at the close with the spectacular 'dump and burn' flyover, the River City.

September 25 - Brisbane Lions lose their attempt for a fourth consecutive Premiership at the AFL Grand Final played in Melbourne against Port Adelaide.

Green house (2000) West End - architects Cottee Parker used tin and timber in addition to concrete to integrate with the character streetscape.

conclusion

Precisely when the public momentum began, to halt the decline of the Brisbane River and repair the damage, is hard to pinpoint. Ironically, it may have been the 1974 floods that first focused the community's attention on the river's failing health. Fingers quickly pointed at the dredging companies when several slippages occurred during and after that flood. The slippage along Coronation Drive was the most serious, causing its closure and subsequent traffic diversion around Land Street. Once the road was reopened, however, the issue quietly dissipated until it disappeared from the public mind. The dredging companies recommenced operations, this time on the new sands carried down by the floodwaters.

Sir Gordon Chalk, then Deputy Premier, had the foresight in the 1970s to fund the ambitious Cultural Centre precinct on the south bank of the river. These were the first public or commercial buildings for several decades which were inclusive of the river. Architect, Robin Gibson, designed the Cultural Centre buildings to take advantage of the river vistas, incorporating a floating fountain and Brisbane's first riverside restaurant (The Fountain Room).

Mainstream impetus to rejuvenate the river gathered pace in the 1980s. Sir Joh Bjelke-Petersen ignored criticism that The World Trade Fair and Exposition would be a white elephant, and

proceeded to promote Expo 88 for the south bank of the river. Within two years of being elected Lord Mayor, Sallyanne Atkinson announced 1987 as Brisbane's "Year of the River". She immediately set up the Lord Mayor's River Strategy Committee, making it clear to developers that public access to the river was essential, and projects should include piazzas, open air dining, ferry landings and boating facilities. The huge success of Expo 88 was the spur for riverside development, as it awoke Brisbane to the potential of its riverfront.

Redevelopment of the historic Eagle Street precinct, with its office towers and riverside walkways, had started in the 1980s with Harry Seidler's Riverside Centre, and will be added to in 2005, when his Riparian Plaza combined office and residential tower is complete. Public access via continuous pedestrian and bicycle pathways on the north bank of the river is now virtually complete, from the Regatta Hotel at Toowong through to Newstead Park at the river's junction with Breakfast Creek.

The Cultural Centre precinct on the south bank of the river will be complete by 2006. The Millennium Arts redevelopment, when finished, will add a Gallery of Modern Art to the existing Queensland Art Gallery and Museum, State Library, Performing Arts Centre, and Conservatorium of Music. On the south bank, riverside parks and walkways presently extend from Orleigh Park at Hill End to Dockside at Kangaroo Point.

The redevelopment of the former Expo site at South Bank has been an outstanding success, with the public thronging to its beach, pools, cafes, and parklands. It has helped Brisbane develop the real sense of community and pride it discovered during Expo 88. Brisbanites frequently flock to South Bank to enjoy outdoor concerts, river fireworks, and other entertainment. It has become the heart of this vibrant city.

South Bank Parklands are complemented by the refurbished Kangaroo Point Cliffs and Parklands, created from the quarrying of the steep wooded hillside that greeted John Oxley and his party on their pioneering journey up the Brisbane River in 1823. A historic galvanised iron Naval Store building, one of a pair erected for the old Queensland Navy, has been recently refurbished and is presently under consideration by the Brisbane City Council for a suitable new use.

Residential riverside redevelopment, which began in the 1990s, gradually replacing the old wharves and industrial sites, has been prolific on both sides of the river. Kangaroo Point, the City, South Brisbane, Newstead, Teneriffe, and New Farm have all seen unprecedented numbers of units, villas, and small lot housing developments. West End's old industrial area is now seeing residential riverside development for the first time in sixty years.

Long serving Lord Mayor Jim Soorley was the first politician with the resolve to stand up to the dredging lobby. He successfully pressured the State Government and, in 1998, they announced that dredging would cease. For the first time since the inception of formal town planning, the river was recognised as a distinct planning entity when "river experience" amendments were introduced by the Soorley Council in 2002. Initiatives to reduce soil run-off from building sites and the filtering of rubbish from storm water drains were also introduced.

The two dominant factors affecting river housing have been the environmental condition of the water and its banks, and the prevailing economic circumstances. The most distinctive river housing was built earlier when the river was virtually unaffected by pollution, industry, and dredging, and again more recently since the river has been on the mend. A clean river and periods of strong economic growth have generally been the catalysts for our most noteworthy river homes.

With public access came the renewed love affair with the river, which now enjoys the full support of our community. Today, the Brisbane River occupies its rightful position as the recreational heart and the spirit of our city. Indeed, the city pays homage to it with the annual River Festival, which draws over 500 000 people to its celebrations and activities.

But we still have a long way to go. Pessimists during the dredging debate questioned whether the river was capable of resurrection. The Great Lakes in North America were pronounced dead in the 1960s, suffering from horrific environmental damage but, after a concerted effort, and time, the lakes have returned to be a recreation and sporting mecca. In the four years since the cessation of dredging, and with increased pollution vigilance, the river has already shown a significant visual improvement. Its water and banks, given time and even more effort, can be further rehabilitated, so that fishing and swimming from sandy beaches will hopefully become commonplace again on the Brisbane River.

Patrick Dixon

There's a river somewhere that flows through the lives of everyone

Roberta Flack

bibliography

Allom, Richard.
The Small Brisbane House pp 19-22

Brewer, F. J. and Dunn, R.
Sixty Years of Municipal Government
(Brisbane: n.p., 1925)

Bryans, T. H.
The Commercial Wharves in The Brisbane
River: A Source-Book for the Future
pp 265-269

Cole, John R.
Shaping A City: 1925-1985
(Brisbane: William Brooks, 1984)

Cossims, Geoffrey.
"Surface Hydrology, Water Supply and
Flooding" in The Brisbane River:
A Source-Book for the Future pp 55-62

Davie, P. Stock, E. and Low Choy, D. eds.
The Brisbane River: A Source-Book for
the Future (Brisbane: Australian Littoral
Society, 1990)

De Gruchy, Graham.
Architecture in Brisbane
(Bowen Hills: Boolarong Publication, 1988)

Fisher, Rod.
"The Brisbane River Personified: Historical
Perception since 1823" in The Brisbane
River: A Source-Book for the Future
pp 183-190

Fisher, Rod and Crozier, Brian.
The Queensland House: a roof over our
heads (Queensland Museum, 1994)

Gibson, Robin.
Life Style and the Built Environment,
(Brisbane: Aquinas Library, 1981)

Glaser, W. and C.
Floating Down the World's Great Rivers
(http://www.sallys-place.com/travel
/world_rivers/rivers_menu.htm)

Goodsir-Cullen, D. J.
"A Working Port" in Seeing Brisbane
1881-2001

Graylard, Geoff.
The Moreton Bay Courier to
The Courier-Mail 1846-1992
(Brisbane: Portside Editions, 1992)

Gregory, Helen.
The Brisbane River Story: Meanders
Through Time (Brisbane: Australian Marine
Conservation Society, 1996)

Hogan, Janet.
The Elite Brisbane House pp 23-27

Hogan, Janet.
Historic Homes of Brisbane
(The National Trust of Queensland, 1979)

Holmes, James.
"Meanders, Reaches, Bights, and Pockets: The Influence of a Serpentine River" in The Brisbane River: A Source-Book for the Future (Australian Littoral Society INC) pp 253-255

Holmes, John.
"The Environment Shaped by Humans: An Overview" in The Brisbane River: A Source-Book for the Future (Australian Littoral Society INC) pp 169-174

Job, William.
The Building of Brisbane: 1828-1940 (St Lucia: University of Queensland Press, 2002)

Job, William.
Brisbane House Styles

Job, William.
Brisbane Historical Buildings: 1828-1940

Job, William.
Early Queensland Architects

McBryde, G. John Oxley.
(http://members.ozemail.com.au/~gmc brydede/explorer/johnoxley.html)

McLeod, Roderick G.
"Some Aspects of the History of the Brisbane River" in The Brisbane River: A Source-Book for the Future pp 191-202

O'Flynn, Michael, and Thornton, Mark.
"Sand, Gravel and Coal Resources of the Brisbane River and Adjacent Areas" in The Brisbane River: A Source-Book for the Future pp 29-41

Pitts, David.
"Recreation in the Brisbane River" in The Brisbane River: A Source-Book for the Future pp 339-358

Ramsay, Kenneth.
Brisbane's Inter-war Suburban Character: A Methodology for Survey and Assessment (Thesis, University of Queensland,1992)

Robinson, Noel J.
Dalton Houses 1956-1975: An exemplar for Brisbane's domestic architects. (Thesis, University of Queensland, 1976)

Saini, Bal.
"The Brisbane House in Environmental Context" in The Brisbane River: A Source-Book for the Future pp 35-42

Sharna, Pramod.
"Social Geography of Catchment Settlements and Riverside Suburbs" in The Brisbane River: A Source-Book for the Future pp 225-242

Stock, Errol.
"Physical Environment on the Brisbane River: An Overview" in The Brisbane River: A Source-Book for the Future pp 3-6

Sumner, Ray.
"The Brisbane House in Historical Context" pp 29-34

Watson, Don.
"An Overview of the Brisbane House" pp 11-17